OXFORD
UNIVERSITY PRESS

Fiona Beddall • Kenna Bourke

Blue Dot 5

Workbook

1 How do people demonstrate intelligence?

A Match to make sentences.

1 If you have good social skills, …
2 If you use good logic, …
3 If you have an advantage in a competition, …
4 If you are an emotional person, …
5 If you make a contribution, …
6 If you have high ability, …

a you can win more easily than other people.
b you can do something well.
c you can solve difficult problems.
d people will thank you for your help.
e you have strong feelings about things.
f you can make friends easily.

B Check (✓) the correct option.

1 There are many ways to demonstrate … intelligence.
☐ naturalistic   ☐ multiple

2 Are you … of writing exciting stories?
☐ develop   ☐ capable

3 Painting can help you to … visual-spatial intelligence.
☐ engage   ☐ develop

4 Can you communicate in … languages or just one?
☐ multiple   ☐ naturalistic

5 Good … skills will help you to talk to people from around the world.
☐ capable   ☐ linguistic

6 If you … with people from different countries, you can learn a lot.
☐ linguistic   ☐ engage

1

A **Write a synonym that can replace the underlined word in each sentence. Use words from the other sentences.**

1 It was a very <u>amusing</u> movie. _funny_

2 Those horses are very <u>fast</u>. _______________

3 That cheese tastes <u>horrible</u>! _______________

4 I laughed at his <u>funny</u> costume. _______________

5 The weather was <u>awful</u>. _______________

6 What <u>fantastic</u> news! _______________

7 It's a <u>quick</u> journey by train. _______________

8 I've had a <u>great</u> day. _______________

B **Complete the sentences with the present perfect of the verbs in parentheses.**

1 You _______________ (make) a big contribution to the project.

2 She _______________ (never, play) a musical instrument.

3 _______________ (they, give) you any help?

4 We _______________ (not do) enough research.

5 Which countries _______________ (he, visit)?

6 I _______________ (learn) a lot of science in school this year.

7 _______________ (you, ever, teach) a friend how to do something?

8 The new table tennis club at school _______________ (not start) yet.

C **Read and circle the correct option.**

We have [1] **been** / **be** hiking all day. At first, the weather was great, but it [2] **have** / **'s** been raining for an hour. I've [3] **being** / **been** wearing a raincoat since the rain started, so I haven't been [4] **got** / **getting** wet. My dad [5] **is** / **has** not been wearing a raincoat, and my mom's raincoat is too small for her. They [6] **haven't** / **aren't** been enjoying the last hour!

D Complete the dialogues with the present perfect continuous of the verbs in parentheses.

1 **A:** You have paint in your hair!
What ________________________ (you, do)?

 B: I ________________________ (paint) a picture.

2 **A:** Where's Fatma?

 B: She ________________________ (rest) in bed all day.
She ________________________ (not feel) well.

3 **A:** Why ________________________ (it, snow) so much?

 B: I don't know, but I hope it stops soon. I ________________________ (stay)
inside all the time to keep warm, and I'm really bored.

4 **A:** You look very hot and tired. ________________________ (you, play) basketball?

 B: No, I ________________________ (run). I ran for 20 minutes without stopping!

E Write a reason. Use the present perfect continuous.

1 Why is Toyama tired?

Because he ____ .

2 Why are André and Sofia wet?

Because they ____ .

3 Why is Chantelle wearing a funny costume?

Because she ____ .

F Read and complete the paragraph.

> have tried   have been trying   haven't made
> haven't been making   have read   have been reading

This week, I [1] ________________________ an interesting book about
intelligence. I [2] ________________________ half of the book so far.
It has a lot of puzzles in it. I [3] ________________________ some of the
puzzles, and they weren't too difficult. But I [4] ________________________
to find the answer to one of the logic problems for days, and I [5] ________________________
much progress. I've checked my math again and again, and I [6] ________________________
a mistake with that. But something isn't right. I'll have to keep trying!

A Read the magazine article. What types of intelligence does it talk about?

The Concert: Musical Intelligence and More

You have taken your seat for the concert, and your favorite musicians have started to perform! They're famous for their musical ability, of course. But multiple types of intelligence have made a contribution to your experience of this fantastic concert tonight. Let's take a look.

First, look at the people on stage. The drummer has been hitting the drums so fast that you can't see his drumsticks. He needs musical intelligence to keep the rhythm, but he also needs physical intelligence to be capable of moving the drumsticks like that. The guitarist needs physical intelligence, too, so she can move her fingers to play the right notes and chords.

There's a slow, sad song now. Can you hear the feeling in the singer's voice? He needs emotional intelligence to perform like that. The songwriter needed emotional intelligence as well as musical intelligence to write a song that communicates those sad feelings so well.

Linguistic intelligence has also contributed to this performance. The songwriter had to be good with words to write the beautiful lyrics. And the band members needed good linguistic intelligence as well as musical intelligence to discuss with each other how to make the performance as good as possible.

But that's not all. Your family bought tickets for the concert online. Who did the math to decide how much the tickets should cost so that there was enough money to pay all the workers at the concert? People with strong logical intelligence. It took excellent logical intelligence to design the sound system for the concert, too, and to make the music sound as good as possible.

There are special lights and screen images to make the performance on stage look exciting. People with great visual-spatial intelligence designed those. And what about the huge room where you're sitting? Without an architect with visual-spatial intelligence to design it, that amazing building wouldn't be there!

A concert performance needs all these different types of intelligence to succeed. But there's another person at the concert who is demonstrating intelligence, too: you. It's a sign of your own musical intelligence that you can enjoy the performance tonight. So have fun, and feel smart!

B **Underline these words in the text.**

contribution   multiple   linguistic   capable   ability   emotional   logic

C **Answer any questions you can without re-reading. Then re-read the article and answer the other questions.**

1 Why do people need physical intelligence? Write two examples from the article.

____

2 Why did the songwriter need emotional intelligence?

____

3 Why did the band members need linguistic intelligence?

____

4 What math did people do before anyone could buy tickets?

____

5 What is only there because of visual-spatial intelligence?

____

6 What does someone in a concert audience need if they want to enjoy the music?

____

D **What types of intelligence does the article say these people demonstrate?**

1 guitarist: _______________, _______________, _______________

2 singer: _______________, _______________, _______________

3 drummer: _______________, _______________, _______________

4 songwriter: _______________, _______________, _______________

5 architect: _______________

6 sound system designer: _______________

A Complete the sentences.

dance routine   shape   from scratch   calculation   visualize   workshop

1 He could ________________ the dragon in the story.

2 Their ________________ was fantastic!

3 She did the ________________ on the board.

4 It's fun making pasta ________________.

5 He went to his ________________ to make some new pots.

6 She can ________________ sand into beautiful sculptures of animals.

B Complete the posters.

handle   dance routine   athletic   visualize   workshop

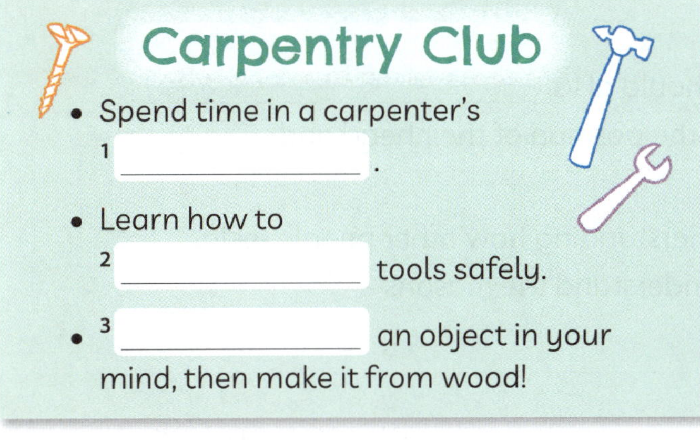

A **Check (✓) the correct option.**

1 I felt really … when my friends went to the beach without me.

☐ clue ☐ upset ☐ behavior

2 He walked slowly, with his head down. I knew from his … that he was tired.

☐ empathy ☐ behavior ☐ body language

3 We searched the room and looked for … .

☐ clues ☐ upset ☐ aware

4 Our … is always good in this class.

☐ behavior ☐ upset ☐ body language

5 Before I found out about his pet lizard, I wasn't … of his love of reptiles.

☐ empathy ☐ clue ☐ aware

6 I felt a lot of … for the characters in the book. I really cared about what happened to them.

☐ empathy ☐ aware ☐ body language

B **Read and complete the paragraphs.**

clue   behavior   upset   be aware of   empathy   body language

1 A smile is a _________________________ that someone is happy. But sometimes people pretend to smile when they are _________________________ because they want to hide their real feelings.

2 People's faces often show their feelings, but we should also _________________________ their _________________________ – for example, the position of their head and how they move their arms.

3 Showing _________________________ means understanding how other people feel. We can be a better friend to people if we try to understand the reasons for their _________________________ .

① Writing Study

A Join the two sentences to make one sentence. Use a comma and one of these conjunctions.

1 I like math puzzles. My sister hates them.

<u>I like math puzzles, but my sister hates them.</u>

2 Zeki is very musical. She has good social skills, too.

____

3 Filip can visualize cool new clothes. He finds fashion design easy.

____

4 I grow a lot of vegetables. I'm not interested in growing flowers.

____

B Rewrite the sentence so it has a semicolon.

1 Mima likes shaping wood into sculptures, but Kalisha prefers painting.

<u>Mima likes shaping wood into sculptures; Kalisha prefers painting.</u>

2 I'm not very athletic, so sports are hard for me.

____

3 Logical intelligence is important in chess, and it's important in a lot of other board games, too.

____

4 He is good at math, but he finds history difficult.

____

C Write a paragraph about the different types of intelligence your friends and family have and how they use them. Use commas and semicolons.

My dad has high emotional intelligence; I know he'll always listen if there's something that's worrying me. My sister isn't as good as Dad at listening to people's problems, but she has fantastic linguistic intelligence. She loves telling stories, and she writes very good poems.

____

____

____

____

"

A **Read and circle the correct option.**

Friendships are important; they make a big [1] **empathy** / **contribution** / **behavior** to your [2] **linguistic** / **multiple** / **emotional** well-being. But if you move to a new school or area, you may need to make new friendships from [3] **scratch** / **shape** / **engage**. This will be a lot easier if you have good [4] **social skills** / **dance routines** / **body language**.

Good social skills are also useful for teamwork. If people in the team disagree, you can use your emotional intelligence to solve the problems, so no one will be [5] **handle** / **clue** / **upset**.

So always look for ways to develop your [6] **ability** / **capable** / **athletic** to communicate well with other people. It can give you a big [7] **logic** / **calculation** / **advantage** in life.

B **Match the categories to the examples.**

1 clues •
2 body language •
3 athletic people •
4 linguistic skills •

• **a** runners and gymnasts
• **b** hugging and smiling
• **c** reading and speaking
• **d** a fingerprint and a hair on a coat

C **Complete the sentences with the correct form of the verb.**

	Present Perfect	Present Perfect Continuous
1 learn	I _____________ hundreds of English words.	I _____________ English for four years.
2 sleep	He _____________ under the stars in the desert.	He _____________ all morning, but he should wake up now.
3 not do	We _____________ enough work on the project yet.	We _____________ enough work on the project this week.
4 write	How many books _____________ (she)?	_____________ (she) her book today?

Think and Reflect: Unit 1

My understanding of intelligence ☆☆☆☆☆
The most interesting thing that I learned _____________
My goal for Unit 2 _____________

2 When do animals use intelligence?

A Complete the sentences.

> bury   figure out   hang   yell   sweep   balance

1 The clothes will dry if you _______________ them on a clothesline.

2 I love to _______________ puzzles.

3 We _______________ the floor every day.

4 I had to _______________ to make him hear me.

5 It's easier to _______________ if you spread your arms wide.

6 At the beach, we sometimes _______________ Dad in the sand!

B Match the definitions to the words or phrases.

1 You might have a pile of these on your desk.   •

2 These are delicious when they're ripe.   •

3 This sometimes causes trouble for transportation.   •

4 This creates warmth.   •

5 You might see this on the end of a pole.   •

6 This is mischievous behavior.   •

- • **a** a lot of snow
- • **b** books
- • **c** apples
- • **d** a monkey taking food from your picnic
- • **e** the sun
- • **f** a flag

A Complete the sentences with their *-ous* adjective forms.

> fury   adventure   ~~fame~~   mountain   mystery
> nerve   envy   poison   humor   vary

1 Even _____famous_____ actors who have appeared in a lot of movies feel _____________ before they perform in a play.

2 Switzerland is a very _____________ country, so it's a great place for _____________ people who enjoy sports like climbing and skiing.

3 He received a _____________ letter in the mail. It didn't say who it was from, but it told him not to eat the apples on his tree because they were _____________ .

4 I feel _____________ of the lucky people who live in sunny places. We have _____________ types of weather here, from gentle rain to snowstorms, but we don't often see the sun.

5 I sent my grandma a _____________ card for her birthday, but sadly the joke on the card upset her. She was _____________ about it!

B Complete the sentences with the simple present or present continuous of the verbs in parentheses.

1 I _____________ (read) an interesting book about owls at the moment.

2 Writers often _____________ (tell) stories about intelligent owls.

3 In fact, owls _____________ (have) a small brain for their body size.

4 My brother sometimes _____________ (see) an owl in our yard at night.

5 I can't sleep right now because an owl _____________ (make) a loud noise near my bedroom window.

C Correct the mistakes. Use the simple past or past continuous.

1 Last fall, a squirrel often <u>comes</u> into our yard to bury nuts.

____

2 One day, it <u>digging</u> a hole for a nut when a fox arrived.

____

3 I saw the fox while I <u>were doing</u> the dishes in the kitchen.

____

4 Suddenly, the fox <u>leap</u> at the squirrel.

____

5 The squirrel quickly <u>climbing</u> a tree.

____

D **Unscramble the sentences.**

1 been / for hours / The hawk / has / sitting / on the branch

____

2 I / been / the birds / feeding / this winter / have

____

3 has / finished / The TV show / about squirrels

____

4 have / never / I / a hummingbird / seen

____

5 of wildlife / been / taking photos / has / today / She

____

E **Read and circle the correct option.**

1 Two hundred years ago, when plenty of gray squirrels **were living** / **have lived** in North America, only red squirrels lived in the forests of Europe.

2 In the 1800s, people **started** / **are starting** to bring gray squirrels to Europe.

3 Since the 1800s, the number of gray squirrels in Europe **grows** / **has been growing**.

4 Gray squirrels **eat** / **are eating** the same food as red squirrels, and they are better at getting the food.

5 In parts of Europe with a lot of gray squirrels today, red squirrels **were disappearing** / **have disappeared**.

6 At the moment, experts **tried** / **are trying** to stop the spread of gray squirrels in Europe to protect red squirrels.

F **Complete the sentences with the correct form of *fly*.**

1 **Simple present:** The bird ________________________ to Alaska every year.

2 **Present continuous:** Look! The bird ________________________!

3 **Simple past:** Last year, the bird ________________________ to Alaska.

4 **Past continuous:** The bird ________________________ when I saw it.

5 **Present perfect:** The bird ________________________ to Alaska five times.

6 **Present perfect continuous:** The bird ________________________ for weeks.

A Read the wildlife story. What was the problem and how did they solve it?

Brainy and the Trash

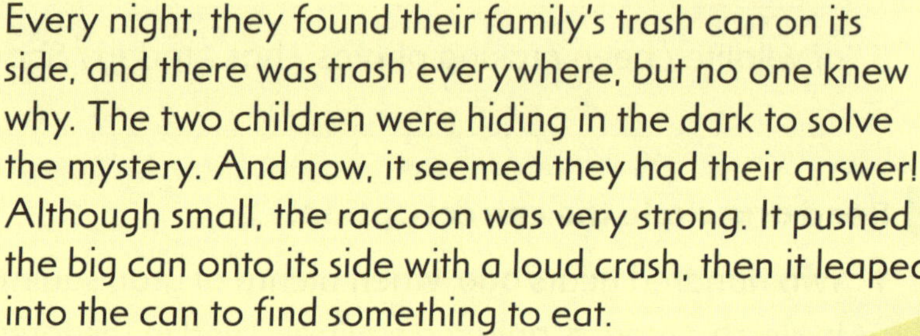

Under a streetlight, a small animal was moving. It had a black and white face and a stripy tail. "It's a raccoon!" said Jaden quietly to Emma.

Every night, they found their family's trash can on its side, and there was trash everywhere, but no one knew why. The two children were hiding in the dark to solve the mystery. And now, it seemed they had their answer! Although small, the raccoon was very strong. It pushed the big can onto its side with a loud crash, then it leaped into the can to find something to eat.

"Hey! Go away!" yelled the children. The raccoon ran off into the night.

The next day, Emma and Jaden put a big rock in the bottom of the trash can. "It'll be too heavy for the raccoon now!" said Jaden.

That night, the children hid again. When the mischievous raccoon arrived, it couldn't push the trash can over. *We've solved the problem!* thought the children happily.

But the raccoon had other ideas. It found a long wooden pole nearby. *What's it doing?* wondered the children.

The raccoon tried again and again to balance the pole against the trash can. On its seventh try, it succeeded, and it climbed up the pole. Then it opened the trash can with its little fingers, and climbed onto the pile of trash inside.

This time, Emma and Jaden were too fascinated to yell at the raccoon.

"It's so intelligent!" smiled Jaden.

"We should call it Brainy!" said Emma.

The next day, Mom put some rope around the trash can to keep the lid down. That night, Brainy's little fingers played with the knot in the rope for about ten minutes. Then the rope fell to the ground, and the raccoon climbed into the can.

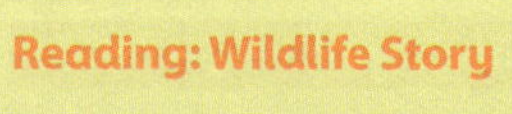

"Brainy is so smart!" laughed Jaden.

The next morning, Mom said, "Maybe we've been trying something impossible. Brainy's too intelligent for this old trash can! I'm going to buy a special new can that raccoons can't open."

Two nights later, the children watched as Brainy tried, and failed, to figure out a way into the new can. Then the raccoon moved on up the street to another house. "Goodbye, Brainy!" said the children. "And good luck!"

B Underline these words in the text.

pile　mischievous　pole　figure out　balance　yell

C Answer the questions.

1 Why are the children hiding at the beginning of the story?

____

4 How does Brainy use the wooden pole?

____

2 Why is Brainy interested in the trash?

____

5 What does Mom use to try to stop Brainy getting into the old trash can?

____

3 Why do the children put a stone in the trash can?

____

6 Why does Brainy go to another house at the end of the story?

____

D Visualize these parts of the wildlife story. Describe the pictures that you see in your mind.

1 Brainy pushing the old trash can onto its side

____

2 Brainy carrying the wooden pole

____

3 Brainy trying to open the new trash can

____

What mischievous animals do you know?
How are they mischievous?

A **Match to make sentences.**

1 Octopus skin usually has a smooth, soft …   a escape.
2 The fish live in a big, glass …   b independently.
3 I didn't need any help. I did it …   c tank.
4 The fox found a nice place to build its …   d resourceful.
5 The crab is inside a large container. It can't …   e texture.
6 The raccoon used a stick to get to the food. It was very …   f den.

B **Read and complete the paragraph.**

located   gap   tank   escape   resourceful

We tested the intelligence of different species of fish. To do this, we put them in a small container ¹ ______________ inside a big ² ______________ of water. There was a small ³ ______________ and a difficult route to ⁴ ______________ from the container. We recorded how long the different fish took to figure out the route. The difference between the speed of the fastest and slowest fish was bigger each time they did the challenge. This was probably because the most intelligent and ⁵ ______________ fish remembered the route from before.

A **Check (✓) the correct option.**

1 The kitten was really … .

☐ fake   ☐ fluffy

2 I'm trying to … this nut.

☐ report   ☐ break open

3 These plants are … . Their leaves are plastic.

☐ fake   ☐ fluffy

4 The … crossed the street at the traffic light.

☐ pedestrians   ☐ entrance

5 My friend was waiting for me at the school … .

☐ pedestrians   ☐ entrance

6 I'm happy to … that our local hedgehog has had babies!

☐ report   ☐ break open

B **Complete the paragraphs.**

entrance   fluffy   fake   break open   pedestrians   report

1 The lid of the tank is open, and the lizard is gone! Did someone _______________ the tank? I should _______________ this to the manager of the animal park!

2 My friend has a new pet rabbit with _______________ black fur. I wanted to walk to her house and play with it, but my mom said no. There's no sidewalk on her road, so it's too dangerous for _______________ .

3 Here's a picture of my brother at the _______________ to the bat cave. His smile is so _______________ ! He's really bad at smiling naturally for a picture!

A Complete the charts.

	Simple Present	Simple Past
1	feel	felt
2		taught
3	make	
4		did
5	hear	

	Simple Present	Simple Past
6		thought
7	say	
8		spoke
9	find	
10		had

B Complete the sentences with irregular simple past verbs from **A**.

1 I ________________ so happy yesterday when I ________________ the good news about the dolphins!

2 I ________________ birds weren't very smart, but last week my teacher ________________ that they can be really intelligent!

3 After my class ________________ a project on animal intelligence, I ________________ my pet parrot to wave at me.

4 Last night I ________________ out about a famous gorilla named Koko. I saw a video about her. She ________________ to humans in sign language!

5 I ________________ a new birdfeeder from wood last Saturday, and yesterday I saw six birds eating from it! I ________________ a great time watching them!

C Write a paragraph from a story about an intelligent animal. Use verbs in the correct tense.

All the elephants felt thirsty. *We must go to Black Lake*, thought Daisy, the oldest elephant in the herd. *I went there many times when I was young, and there was always water there.*

The elephants slowly made the journey to Black Lake. It was a long way, but Daisy found the lake easily. She remembered all the journeys from her younger years.

But when they arrived, they heard a very strange noise. What was happening?

____

____

____

____

A **Unscramble the words to complete the paragraph.**

Can you see that tree in the ¹ g_____________ (apg) between the houses? Every summer, ² r_____________ (prei) peaches ³ h_____________ (hgan) from its branches. I love the soft ⁴ t_____________ (xtreetu) of their skin, and their sweet taste. At the moment, there are also some baby birds with ⁵ f_____________ (ulffyf) feathers in the tree. Their ⁶ r_____________ (uleroucfres) mother has been teaching them to fly today, by taking food to a nearby branch and calling them to it.

B **Read and circle the correct option.**

Foxes can be very beautiful, but when they come to our yard, they cause a lot of ¹ **pole** / **trouble** / **pile**. It's really annoying! They don't like the ² **warmth** / **gap** / **entrance** of the day, so they usually come at night, when it's colder. They often ³ **yell** / **break open** / **escape** the trash bags and the trash goes everywhere. It's always my job to ⁴ **report** / **figure out** / **sweep** the path and make it clean after they've visited. I've read that they ⁵ **fake** / **bury** / **balance** food from trash cans somewhere near their ⁶ **den** / **pedestrian** / **mischievous** so they can eat it later.

C **Match to make sentences.**

1 Last year, the seabirds …
2 At the moment, the dolphins …
3 The squirrels aren't hungry because they …
4 The elephant has never …
5 We saw a bear when we …

a were walking in the forest.
b started to use stones to break open shellfish.
c have been eating all day.
d been here before.
e are playing a game.

Think and Reflect: Unit 2

My understanding of intelligence ☆☆☆☆☆

How well I achieved my goal for Unit 2 ☆☆☆☆☆

The most interesting thing that I learned _______________________________

My goal for Unit 3 _______________________________

Vocabulary 1

A Circle the correct option.

1 Digitial devices use **artificial** / **navigate** intelligence to think.

2 Cellphones let us **code** / **interact** with other people anywhere, by text or voice.

3 This GPS system helps us to **recognize** / **navigate** to places.

4 This **code** / **calculate** tells the computer what to do.

5 This phone can **drone** / **recognize** its owner's face.

6 This **drone** / **interact** is flying above the field to make a video.

B Read and complete the advertisement.

> instantly   data   device   calculate   stream   time-consuming

Do you ever think a snail might complete a marathon in the time that you can ¹ ______________ your favorite show? The SpeedyGizmo can solve your problem! It can ² ______________ large quantities of ³ ______________ quickly, so you can relax and enjoy the show.

I was experiencing ⁴ ______________ delays when I was trying to watch shows. Now, with my SpeedyGizmo, I click on the show that I want to watch, and ⁵ ______________ it starts to play. It's an amazing ⁶ ______________ . I recommend the SpeedyGizmo to everyone!

SpeedyGizmo – for people who can't wait

Which device do you use the most regularly?

Word Study and Grammar

A **Complete the sentences with these verbs or their *-ion* noun forms.**

> construct   connect   educate   invent   collect
> navigate   translate   communicate

1 I ________________ toy robots. I have a robot astronaut, a robot dancer, and a lot more.
I love my robot ________________!

2 They're going to ________________ some new buildings at our school, but the work will take
years. I'll probably be at a different school before the ________________ has finished.

3 My father is working on a ship at the moment, so ________________ is difficult. We try to
talk every week, but we don't always get a good Internet ________________. It's frustrating
trying to ________________ with someone when the technology isn't working properly.

4 I have had a good ________________, with the opportunity to learn three different
languages. I can speak them well, but I can't ________________ from one language to
another very quickly. ________________ is definitely difficult for me.

5 It's possible to use the stars to help you ________________ at night, but ________________
has been much easier since the ________________ of GPS devices.

B **Complete the chart.**

	Simple Past	Simple Present	Future with *will*
1	I could sing.	I can sing.	
2		He can't navigate.	
3			We'll be able to swim.
4	They couldn't write.		
5			It won't be able to drive.
6		You can translate.	

can   could   will be able to   can't   couldn't   won't be able to

In the 1980s, people didn't have the Internet at home, so they [1] _______________ stream videos. Instead, they [2] _______________ borrow a video from a video store, watch it on their TV at home, and take it back to the store the next morning.

These days, you [3] _______________ find many video stores because most of them have closed. But that doesn't matter, because you [4] _______________ choose something interesting to watch at home without leaving your living room. The popularity of video streaming won't continue forever. In the future, we [5] _______________ watch our favorite shows using new types of technology. The children of the future [6] _______________ imagine a world with only the technology that we use today!

D **Look and write sentences about the robot.**

speak   carry the groceries   play the violin   cook

1 It will be able to carry the groceries. _______________

2 _______________

3 _______________

4 _______________

E **Write three sentences about what you *could* and *couldn't* do when you were five. Then write three sentences about what you *will* and *won't be able to* do when you're older.**

1 _______________

2 _______________

3 _______________

4 _______________

5 _______________

6 _______________

A Look at the three headings and think of a question for each one.
Read the website article and find the answers.

who   what   where   when   why   how

AI: A SMART FUTURE

A lot of people are talking about artificial intelligence — AI — and how it's going to change the world. But what will these changes look like? Let's look at AI's possible impact on three different areas.

1 Health

At the moment, human carers look after people when they're too ill to take care of themselves, but the future might be very different. Some experts think that, when you're older, you're likely to have a robot carer instead. Robot carers will have code to tell them what to do. They will be able to talk to you, cook for you, and bring things to you.

But there's more. AI may also help you to stay healthy in the first place. Doctors can use AI to study images of people's blood, lungs, or other body parts, and predict who will get particular diseases. Then the doctors can treat patients before the disease makes them unwell. Awesome!

2 Sport

In the past, only humans could decide if an athlete came first in a race, scored a goal, or broke the rules. Now we can use a few cameras in key places to help. But in the future, AI will be able to study data from hundreds of cameras in different places and at different angles, to decide instantly what happened. This will make sport fairer for all the competitors.

Many athletes already wear devices that can measure their body's performance. In the future, AI will be able to use more data from these devices, and recommend more accurately how best to train. This will be normal, not just for high-ability athletes, but for everyone. AI will also be able to recognize when someone's body needs a rest, so fewer people will get hurt when they play sports.

③ Video games

A lot of people love gaming today, but the video games of the future are going to be incredible! With the help of AI, games will be able to recognize your emotional response, and give you a game experience that perfectly matches your emotional needs for that moment. You will have difficulty levels that are exactly right for just you, and different from every other player. And as virtual reality technology develops, you'll interact with a game world that feels completely real.

New technology usually brings a mix of advantages and disadvantages, and AI will be the same. But a lot of the results of AI are going to be so exciting!

B Underline these words in the text.

recognize   data   code   devices   artificial   interact   instantly

C Write your questions for the three headings. Then write the answers you found in the website article. If you didn't find the answers, where might you find them?

1 Q: ____

   A: ____

2 Q: ____

   A: ____

3 Q: ____

   A: ____

D Circle the correct option.

1 Some experts think ill people will get their care from robots **instead of** / **as well as** humans.

2 AI might help doctors to treat patients **when** / **before** they get a disease.

3 AI will be able to study data from a lot of cameras to make games **fairer** / **easier to watch** than now.

4 AI will help athletes to **choose a sport** / **stop before they get hurt**.

5 The video games of the future will be **the same** / **different** for each player.

6 The world of a game will feel more **challenging** / **real** than it feels now.

What changes from AI do you think will be the most exciting in the future? Why?

A **Check (✓) the correct option.**

1 Drive carefully so you don't have an … .

☐ obstacle ☐ accident

2 Should I walk or take the bus? I can't make a … !

☐ decision ☐ sensor

3 The journey took longer than normal today, because there was a lot of … .

☐ traffic congestion ☐ program

4 I'd love a job in AI – I think it would be … .

☐ responsible ☐ fascinating

5 When the … notice that it's getting dark, the lights turn on instantly.

☐ sensors ☐ decisions

6 They can … the car to make sure it doesn't drive too fast.

☐ accident ☐ program

B **Read and complete the paragraph.**

accident   decision   obstacle
responsible   sensors   traffic congestion

I love my new quintiped. It's the perfect vehicle when there's [1] _______________________,
because it can walk between the lines of traffic. And it has [2] _______________________
that notice when it's getting near an [3] _______________________ in the road, so it makes a
warning noise before I hit it and cause an [4] _______________________. The quintiped can't
steer itself – I'm [5] _______________________ for that. But I don't mind, because it's very
easy to drive. Getting a quintiped was the best [6] _______________________ of my life!

A **Match to make sentences.**

1 I measured the desk carefully, because … •
2 It took me hours to walk home, because … •
3 There was an earthquake, and … •
4 I took some medicine, and … •
5 I'm interested in human biology, so … •
6 I broke my leg two months ago, but … •

• **a** I got lost in the forest.
• **b** I might become a surgeon.
• **c** it took away the pain in my back.
• **d** the disaster destroyed a lot of homes.
• **e** luckily it has healed now.
• **f** I wanted to be accurate.

B **Read and complete the paragraphs.**

> disaster   surgeon   got lost   healed   pain   accurate

A robot has changed my life! Before I went to the hospital, it was difficult for me to walk fast because I had a lot of [1] ________________ in my knee. Once, when I was out on a walk with my friends, I was too slow for the rest of the group. I [2] ________________ because I couldn't see which way they went. What a [3] ________________ ! It was really scary until they came and found me.

But now my knee problem has disappeared. The [4] ________________ at the hospital used a robot to cut into my knee. The cuts were very [5] ________________ because the robot doesn't make mistakes like humans sometimes do. That wasn't a problem for me. The cuts have [6] ________________ now, and I can walk quickly and easily again. I'm so happy!

A **Read the magazine article. Label the different sections.**

Details   Conclusion   Hook

A Brief History of the Internet

Can you imagine life without the Internet? No video and music streaming. No social media. Nowhere to find information except a library! But we don't have to go too far back in time to discover the early days of the Internet's history. So, when did it start, and why?

In 1958, the U.S. president created an organization called ARPA. Its job was to develop exciting new technologies to help the U.S. ARPA's scientists wanted to find quicker ways to share information. They developed a system that connected computers in different places. They called it ARPANET. In 1969, for the first time, data traveled from one computer to another on this new system. That data was just the first two letters of the word "login". The system crashed before anyone could type the rest of the word! But people were happy because the earliest form of the Internet was born.

The next important step in the Internet's development came in 1989. Tim Berners-Lee, a scientist from a European research organization called CERN, invented the World Wide Web. It allowed any computer around the world to connect to a network and share all sorts of data. Suddenly, information was a lot easier to find.

Things began to move fast after that. From the 1990s, people were buying things online from websites including Amazon and eBay. And in the 2000s, social media websites, such as Facebook and X (formerly known as Twitter), were becoming popular.

The 2000s were also when the smartphone was born. More and more people started to use a smartphone instead of a computer to explore the Internet.

Now, it isn't only computers and smartphones that can connect to the Internet, but cars, watches, and many other devices can, too. The Internet gives us the use of a huge amount of data. It can help us to learn, laugh, communicate, exercise, navigate, and much more. It has changed enormously since its invention, and it has changed the world with it. What do YOU think is its most useful function?

B **Answer the questions.**

1 What makes you interested in reading more?

____

2 What interesting steps in the history of the Internet does the article include?

____

3 How does the conclusion connect the details in the article to the reader's life?

____

C You're going to write a magazine article about the history of another type of technology. Brainstorm. Write your ideas in the graphic organizer below.

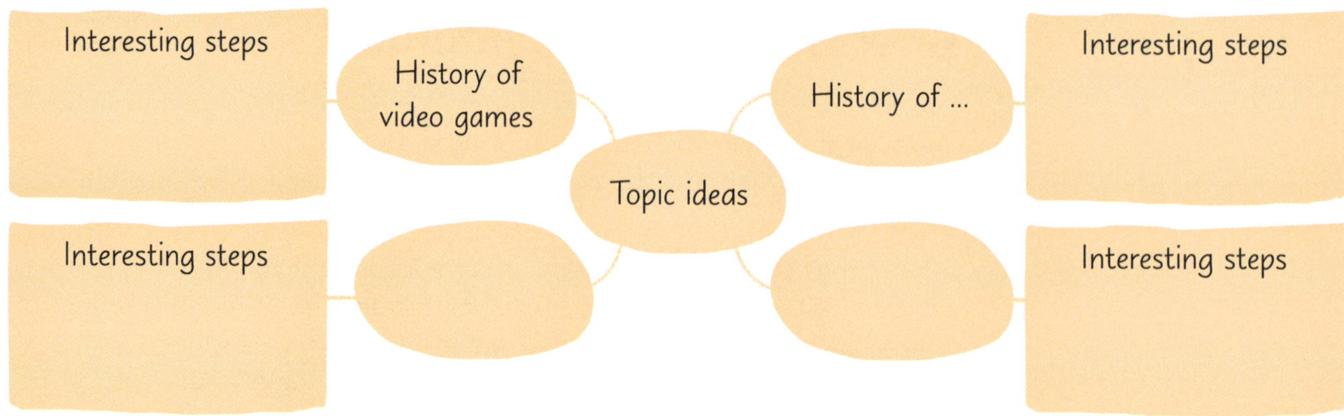

D Do some research and plan your article by completing the chart.

Topic:

Hook:

Step 1:

Step 2:

Step 3:

Step 4:

Conclusion:

E Now write the first draft of your magazine article in your notebook. 

- Start your article with a hook to get the reader interested.
- Include details that you find interesting.
- Write a conclusion that connects the details in your article to the reader's life in some way.

F Check your work and make any necessary changes.

- Did you do everything in the list in **E**?
- Is your grammar, spelling, and punctuation correct?
- Is your writing clear and easy for other people to understand?

G Now write the final draft of your magazine article in your notebook.

A Unscramble the words to complete the dialogues.

1 **A:** We can't go on this road. There's an **¹ o**______________ (closbeta) blocking the route. It's a

fallen tree. It's causing a lot of **² t**______________ (fifcrat) **³ c**______________ (oncstegoni).

B: Let's turn around and go to school on different roads. I can use a map to

⁴ n______________ (vgiantea). I promise we won't **⁵ g**______________ **l**______________ (teg stol).

2 **A:** When my uncle was a child, he didn't **⁶ s**______________ (tamers) music. He listened to things
called CDs that he played on a special machine.

B: It's **⁷ f**______________ (nfiagsctain) how technology has changed! Most devices today can

⁸ c______________ (aelctulca) large amounts of data in just seconds!

B Read and circle the correct option.

My favorite toy is my **¹ sensor / drone / data**. I love flying it when I can find somewhere safe.
I'd like to **² recognize / heal / program** it so it can fly itself. Writing the **³ code / decision / pain** for
that would be difficult and **⁴ instantly / device / time-consuming**! But it would be an interesting
challenge. There's just one problem. If I make a mistake with my code, the drone might fall out of
the sky and cause an **⁵ interact / accident / accurate**. I don't want to be **⁶ responsible / artificial /
instantly** for a **⁷ disaster / calculate / surgeon** like that!

C Look and write sentences.

1 (walk / one year old) <u>She couldn't walk when she was one year old.</u>

2 (ride a bike / now) ____

3 (do this calculation / now) ______________________________________

4 (run fast / 80 years old) ____

Think and Reflect: Unit 3

My understanding of intelligence ☆☆☆☆☆

How well I achieved my goal for Unit 3 ☆☆☆☆☆

The most interesting thing that I learned ____________________________

My goal for Unit 4 ____

Vocabulary 1

A **Look and write the letter.**

1 Snorkeling is a lot of fun. _____

2 Look at it up close! _____

3 I love this when it's fresh. _____

4 It's important to have enough protection. _____

5 That's an interesting statue. _____

6 Look at this abandoned place. _____

B **Circle the correct option.**

1 How do I **attach** / **accomplish** the snorkeling equipment to my head?

2 I always thought he was Brazilian, but **point of view** / **apparently** he's Mexican.

3 They built this strong wall for protection against their **locations** / **enemies** .

4 She's young, but she's already **apparently** / **accomplished** a lot of things in her life.

5 From this **point of view** / **attach** up on a hill, the town looks tiny.

6 This is a fantastic **location** / **enemy** for a vacation.

A Match with the words that mean the same as the underlined phrases.

1 The building was <u>incredibly old</u>. •
2 I saw a <u>very small</u> spider. •
3 It was <u>extremely cold</u> outside! •
4 His jokes were <u>very funny</u>. •
5 She was <u>extremely angry</u> that I borrowed her bike without asking her. •
6 It's <u>incredibly hot</u> out in the sun today! •
7 Russia is an <u>extremely big</u> country. •
8 That's a <u>very interesting</u> idea. •

• **a** hilarious
• **b** tiny
• **c** ancient
• **d** boiling
• **e** furious
• **f** huge
• **g** fascinating
• **h** freezing

B Read and write *a*, *b*, or *c* for the underlined sentences.

a sure that something is true
b sure that something isn't true
c not sure if something is true or not true

1 The statue looks modern. <u>It can't be hundreds of years old.</u> _____
2 That bird's too small to be an eagle. <u>It might be a hawk.</u> _____
3 Look at these symbols. <u>They must be writing!</u> _____
4 You have a big purple bruise on your leg. <u>That has to hurt!</u> _____
5 She knows a lot about planes. <u>She might be a pilot.</u> _____
6 He doesn't speak a word of Spanish. <u>He can't live in Spain.</u> _____

C Read and circle the correct option.

The tree in that photo has a huge trunk. It **¹must / can't** be more than a meter wide! The tree **²has to / might** be in a forest, or it **³might / must** be just one tree on its own.

Oh! It can fit in someone's hands so it **⁴must / can't** be a normal-sized tree. It **⁵must / can't** be tiny. It **⁶has to / can't** be a bonsai tree. We learned about them in school! They're little trees that grow in a pot inside your home.

Would you prefer a pet that's huge or tiny? Why?

have to   has to   might   can't   must

1   The weather's very hot today.

You _______________ be in Antarctica.

2   People here speak English.

You _______________ be in Australia.

3   I can hear waves.

There _______________ be water near you.

4   I'm on the Atlantic coast.

It _______________ be in the Americas,
Europe, or Africa.

5   I'm near New York City.

You _______________ be in the U.S.A.!

E **Read, think, and answer. Use the words in parentheses.**

1   **Laila:**   There are a lot of beds where I work. (might)

Where does Laila work? <u>She might work in a hospital.</u>

2   **Jorge:**   From here, houses and cars look tiny. (might)

Where is Jorge? _______________________________________

3   **Mathilde:**   Everyone in my family speaks French. (must)

What language does Mathilde speak with her family? _______________

4   **Benito and Carlos:**   We've eaten two kilos of tomatoes today. (have / has to)

Do Benito and Carlos like tomatoes? _______________________________

5   **Karim:**   It's snowing in my town! (can't)

Where does Karim live? _____________________________________

6   **Aiko:**   If I look up, I can see a lot of trees. (have / has to)

Where is Aiko? ____

F **Write sentences about one thing that can't be true, one thing that must be true, and one thing that might be true.**

1   ____

2   ____

3   ____

A Read the magazine article. Which animal's perspective did each child use?

Photo Corner

Change Your View!

Did you know, you can have a bird's eye view of something? Or a worm's eye view? The same thing must look very different to a bird flying in the sky and a worm crawling on the ground!

In this week's Photo Corner, we're celebrating fresh perspectives. Like a worm or a bird, the children who took these photos have looked at the world from a point of view that we don't usually see. And their results are fantastic!

Forest trees in the fall

"I love lying on my back in a forest and photographing the trees above me. It's a worm's eye view! I can't be the only person who likes looking at trees from this position. It's fascinating how different tree species make different patterns against the sky, and how the colors and patterns change with the seasons."

Maxim

Rock arch and pyramid in the ocean, with seaweed below

"I enjoy taking underwater photographs when I'm snorkeling, but I get my favorite photos when the camera is only half underwater. It really shows the difference between what you can see above and below the ocean's surface. I think of it as a dolphin's eye view! I took this photo when I was at a location that's famous for the interesting shapes of its rocks. No one ever seems to notice the shapes of seaweed, but they're really interesting too. Dolphins must see some incredible things!"

Diya

"I stood right next to tree trunks and took photos of their bark up close – a squirrel's eye view! I love the diversity of tree bark. I found bark that looks like cracked, dry mud, and bark that looks as if caterpillars are crawling on it. But my favorite bark has layers of different colors and looks like camouflage fabric!"

Chen

Sycamore tree bark

Ash tree bark

Tulip tree bark

View of the River Seine, with the Eiffel Tower on the skyline

B Underline these words in the text.

snorkeling   fresh   location   point of view   statue   up close

C Complete the sentences.

1 The photos are in the article because they all look at the world from ________________.

2 Maxim thinks it's fascinating how ________________ make different patterns.

3 Diya likes to take photos that show the difference between what's above and below ________________.

4 Chen likes ________________ because of its diversity.

5 Charlotte's photo shows a ________________ that people on the ground don't notice.

D  Look at the pictures and captions. Answer the questions.

1 Where and when did Maxim take his photo?

____

2 What's below the ocean in Diya's photo?

____

3 Which species of tree has bark that looks like dry mud?

____

4 Which species of tree has bark that seems to have caterpillars crawling on it?

____

5 What can you see from the top of a famous landmark in Paris?

____

What would you like to photograph for Photo Corner? Why?

4 Vocabulary 2

A Read and complete the blog post.

outline   canvas   shade   three-dimensional   scale   transform

How to Draw a Great Picture

First, decide what you want to draw. Then, choose the surface that you are going to draw on. For example, it could be paper, [1] ______________ , wood, a stone, or even a wall if you want your art to be on a bigger [2] ______________ . Next, draw the [3] ______________ of your picture. When you are happy with the shape that you've drawn, add color. Finally, [4] ______________ the picture to make it darker where there should be shadow. If you do this well, your picture will [5] ______________ into something that looks [6] ______________ .

B Look and circle the correct option.

In picture [1] **A** / **B**, the artist has painted red and purple colors onto a large [2] **shade** / **canvas**. The image [3] **tricks** / **outlines** you into thinking that it is spinning.

Picture [4] **A** / **B** shows a duck. But if you turn the page around and look at the picture from a different [5] **scale** / **angle**, it has [6] **three-dimensional** / **transformed** into a rabbit.

A   **Match to make sentences.**

1   Why is there so much mud on you? You're …   a   covered in it.

2   A mountain path with a lot of stones on it is …   b   crater.

3   The round hole at the top of a volcano is a …   c   mission.

4   We are going to find the secret castle. That's our …   d   bright.

5   The park gets no sunlight because tall buildings …   e   bumpy.

6   It's a warm day today, and the sun is very …   f   surround it.

B   **Complete the sentences.**

covered   surround   crater   mission   bright   bumpy

1   The astronaut's _______________ is to travel to the surface of Mars.

2   She has to land her spaceship inside a big, round _______________.

3   From Mars, Earth looks like a _______________ star in the night sky.

4   Most of Mars is _______________ in orange or brown dust.

5   There are small rocks on Mars, too, so vehicles on the planet have to drive across _______________ surfaces.

6   Some gases _______________ Mars, but humans can't stay alive by breathing Mars's atmosphere.

Writing Study

4

A **Complete the chart with the correct adjectives.**

Colombian   plastic   horrible
round   pink   drinking   new   little

Opinion	Size	Age	Shape	Color	Origin	Material	Purpose

B **Rewrite the sentences with the adjectives in parentheses. Put the adjectives in the correct order.**

1 I'm from a small island. (Greek, flat)

   I'm from a small flat Greek island.

2 Rino has a blue bike. (old, mountain)

   ____

3 Olga loves her tennis clothes. (cotton, loose)

   ____

4 Look at the beautiful flowers! (tall, purple)

   ____

5 It's a gray kitten. (young, cute)

   ____

6 Try one of these chocolate cookies! (square, small)

   ____

C **Write a paragraph about your bedroom, or the perfect bedroom that you would like to have. Use adjectives in the correct order.**

My perfect bedroom has pretty blue walls and large colorful posters of my favorite soccer players. It has a comfortable modern metal bed with a warm blue wool blanket on top. My new wooden baseball bat and my cool red running shoes are next to my desk. The big glass windows make it a nice bright room. It's perfect!

____

____

____

____

A **Read and write *a*, *b*, or *c*.**

1 My favorite thing to do at the beach is _____ . I love seeing fish _____ .

   a canvas **b** snorkeling **c** up close

2 From some _____ , he still looks young, but _____ he's almost sixty.

   a apparently **b** scales **c** angles

3 Our _____ has really challenged us, but we're proud of what we've _____ .

   a accomplished **b** mission **c** abandoned

4 The cave _____ the bears from the sun and gives them _____ from storms.

   a protection **b** shades **c** fresh

B **Unscramble the words to complete the paragraph.**

Jasmin flew her spaceship above the planet's [1] b_____________ (mybpu) surface. It was impossible to land somewhere [2] c_____________ (redcvoe) in rocks like this. But she had almost no fuel. She needed to land … soon! She spotted a [3] c_____________ (etracr) – a huge circle of rock that [4] s_____________ (uosudnderr) a deep, round hole. It was the only possible [5] l_____________ (ticalono) for a landing. Slowly, carefully, she landed the spaceship in the crater, with the [6] b_____________ (gbitrh) lights of her vehicle lighting the way.

C **Read and circle the correct option.**

Dad: Malee, there's a box for you, with a "Thank you!" label on it. It [1] **must** / **can't** have a gift inside.

Malee: Ooo, it [2] **have to** / **must** be from Grandma. I helped her clean her kitchen yesterday.

Dad: Maybe Grandma sent you flowers!

Malee: Yes, but the box is a small flat shape, Dad. It [3] **must** / **can't** have fresh flowers in it!

Dad: It [4] **might** / **can't** be a box of chocolates. Does it make a noise if you shake it?

Malee: Yes, it does! And look, there's the name of a famous chocolate maker on the side of the box. It [5] **might** / **has to** be chocolates. Yum!

Think and Reflect: Unit 4

My understanding of perspective ☆☆☆☆☆

How well I achieved my goal for Unit 4 ☆☆☆☆☆

The most interesting thing that I learned _______________________________________

My goal for Unit 5 _______________________________________

Why do we think differently about the same situation?

Vocabulary 1

A Complete the sentences.

go trampolining   flood   formation   low   stuck   scare

1 My foot is ________________ in the fence.

2 The backyards in my street often ________________.

3 That plane is flying very ________________.

4 I love to ________________ on the weekend.

5 Spiders really ________________ me.

6 That cloud ________________ looks like a rabbit.

B Write something to replace the underlined words, so that the sentences are true for you.

1 I think <u>reading a book</u> is a relaxing activity.   ________________

2 I think <u>lions</u> are terrifying animals.   ________________

3 I always look forward to <u>days with my uncle</u>.   ________________

4 <u>Freezing</u> weather is very common where I live.   ________________

5 I like to entertain myself by <u>writing stories</u>.   ________________

6 It takes me forever to <u>walk to school</u>.   ________________

A **Write the correct compound nouns. Use a word from each box.**

wheel   door   home   soccer   fire   bus   space   hair

cut   ship   stop   bell   fighter   work   chair   shoes

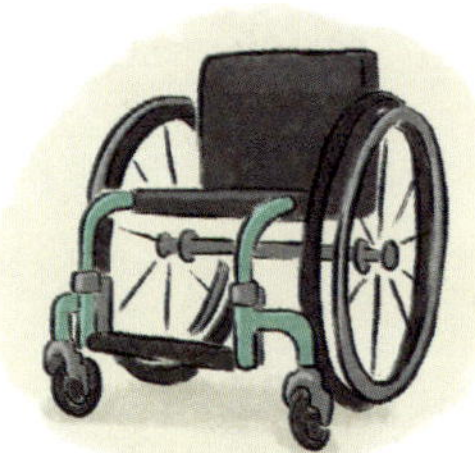

1 _______________

2 _______________

3 _______________

4 _______________

5 _______________

6 _______________

7 _______________

8 _______________

B **Read, think, and complete the facts in the future. Use *will* or *won't* and the verbs.**

lose   start   rise   be   have

1 A new century _______________ on January 1, 2100.

2 The sun _______________ at 3:00 p.m. tomorrow.

3 Many tree species _______________ their leaves next fall.

4 A lot of animals _______________ babies next spring.

5 Next year, I _______________ fifteen years old.

C **Write three predictions about things you believe will be true. Use *will* or *won't*.**

1 What will the weather be like in your country in the future?

____

2 What exciting change will there be in the future?

____

3 How will humans be different in the future?

____

 Complete the future plans. Use the verbs in parentheses and the correct form of *going to*.

1   He ____________________________ (learn) Chinese next year.

2   I ____________________________ (not live) here all my life.

3   They ____________________________ (relax) this afternoon.

4   She ____________________________ (not visit) her grandparents tomorrow.

5   We ____________________________ (not take) the train to school.

6   I ____________________________ (buy) some new jeans soon.

 Match what has happened with your predictions.

1   She's fallen and hit her head. •   • a   He's going to get a good grade.

2   He's been studying hard for the test. •   • b   There's going to be some rain.

3   My little cousin looks tired. •   • c   It's going to hurt tonight.

4   The sky is getting very dark. •   • d   He's going to have an accident.

5   The cars in front of ours have stopped. • • e   She's going to fall asleep soon.

6   That driver is not being careful. •   • f   We're going to be stuck in traffic.

 Complete the sentences with *will* or *going to* and the correct form of the verbs in parentheses.

1   Look at those buds. The plants ____________________________ (have) flowers on them soon.

2   I ____________________________ (see) a movie later. I'm looking forward to it!

3   I'm sure you ____________________________ (love) trampolining. It's such a fun sport.

4   My cousin studies a lot of science because she ____________________________ (work) as a doctor after university.

5   I think she ____________________________ (enjoy) being a doctor.

6   Tomorrow ____________________________ (be) April 10.

What plans do you have for next week?

A Read the online chat. What's the main thing that Lars and Teresa disagree about?

 School-to-School Chat

Saturday

 Hey there, Teresa! How are you? Are you having a nice weekend?

 Hi, Lars! It hasn't been very exciting so far, to be honest. I've been doing homework and chores all day. 😑

 Me too! Life in Mexico and Sweden is very similar! 😔

 But soon I'm going to go trampolining. And after that it'll be dark, so the weekend will get more interesting.

 Why?

 My friend and I borrowed a telescope from my school's science club, and we're going to look at the stars with it. There are no clouds today, so it's going to be a clear night. I absolutely love stargazing. ❤️

 Do you do it a lot?

 Yes. I first tried it six months ago, and now I do it whenever I can. It's so annoying that you can't see the stars during the day, but I always look forward to nighttime.

 Really? I hate the dark.

 Why? Does it scare you? 

 No. It's just that you can't do anything fun in the dark. 😒

 There's a lot that you can do to entertain yourself, even if you don't like stargazing. I love to stay inside and play games 🎮 , read 📕 , see movies 🍿 . And people play sports inside, too. 🏒 ⚽ 🎾

 Sure, but I get bored of all those things, because it's dark so much during the Swedish winter 🌌 . It's dark when we walk to school in the morning, and it's dark when we finish school. There are only a few hours of daylight 🌞 , and we're in class for most of that time. After school, I just want to play outside, but I'm stuck inside every evening instead. 😟 The nights seem to go on forever.

 Try stargazing! It's a wonderful feeling to look at places billions of kilometers away and imagine what they're like. 🪐

I've tried it on vacation, but it isn't easy where I live. In a city, the streetlights don't only light up the streets; they light up the sky too, and that blocks out the starlight. You can see very few stars around here. Honestly, there's nothing good about the dark for me. 😫 But I'm happy that you can enjoy it!

I guess I'm lucky that I live in the country. 😊

And I'm lucky that it'll be spring here soon ☀️. Spring and summer feel really special after the long winter nights. I'm looking forward to country hikes 🏞️ on weekends, and playing with my friends after school 🥳.

B **Underline these words in the text.**

go trampolining   stuck   forever   entertain   scare   look forward to

C **Read and write *True* or *False*.**

1   Teresa has had an exciting day so far. ________________

2   Teresa is going to look at the stars with her school's telescope. ________________

3   Lars is afraid of the dark. ________________

4   Lars lives in Sweden. ________________

5   It isn't easy to stargaze in Lars's city because of the streetlights. ________________

6   At the moment, it's spring where Lars lives. ________________

D  **Compare and contrast Teresa and Lars. Complete the Venn diagram.**

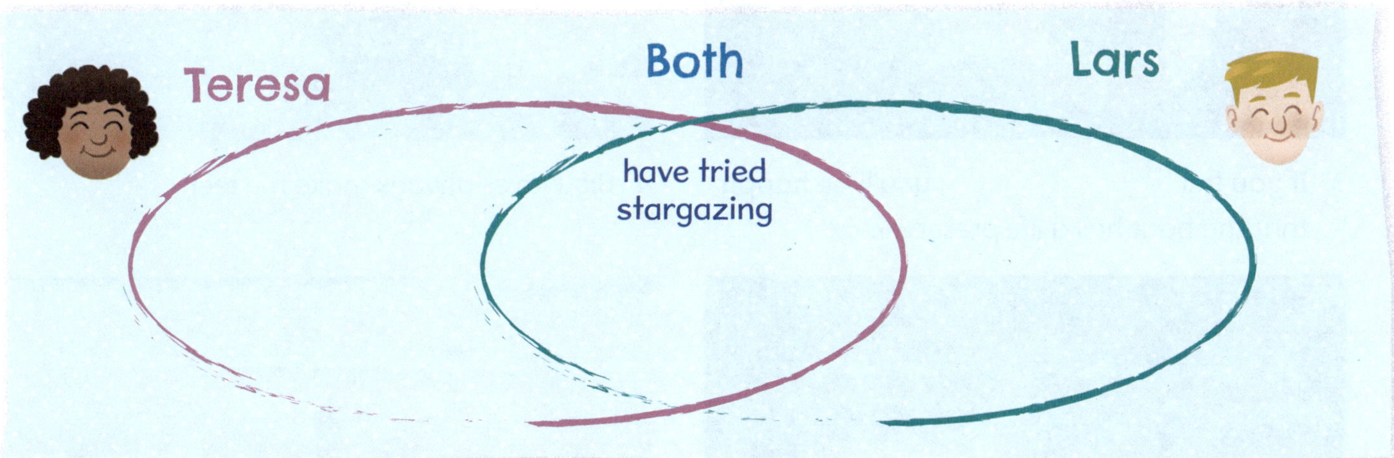

What do you think of the dark?
What do you do on dark evenings?

A **Match to make sentences.**

1 I've run out of water, …
2 I don't have any oars, …
3 I've jumped overboard, …
4 I often get seasick, …
5 I'm on a yacht, …
6 I rescued them, …

a so I can't move the boat.
b so I hate traveling on water.
c so now I'm swimming next to the boat.
d so they want to thank me.
e so I'm going to sleep in a bed in the middle of the ocean.
f so I'm going to be thirsty.

B **Complete the sentences.**

overboard   yacht   stranded   solid   oar   seasick

1 It's a beautiful ________________ but I don't know how to sail it.

2 Water is liquid, but ice is ________________.

3 If you fall ________________, you'll be happy that the boat has a life preserver.

4 Big waves always make me feel ________________.

5 If you pull your ________________ harder, we'll go faster.

6 I can't get off this island. I'm ________________.

A Read and circle *True* or *False*.

1 An annual event happens every month. — **True** **False**

2 A cavity is good for a tooth. — **True** **False**

3 People sometimes need a filling when there's a problem with their tooth. — **True** **False**

4 People often sit in a waiting room before they see a doctor or dentist. — **True** **False**

5 People only have a checkup if they are very worried about their health. — **True** **False**

6 If you chip a plate or cup, it doesn't look new anymore. — **True** **False**

B Read and complete the dialogue.

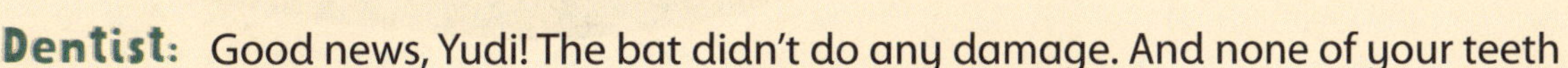

> cavity   waiting room   checkup   annual   filling   chip

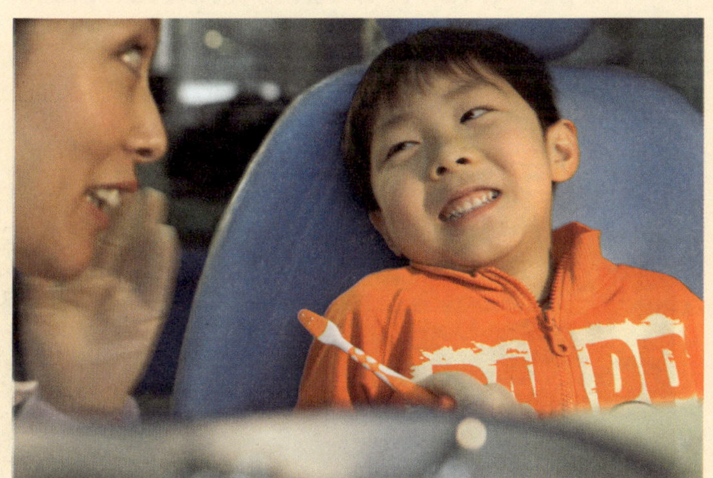

Dentist: Hello, Yudi. Have you been having any tooth problems recently?

Yudi: Hello, Dr. Lee. Yes. I had an accident with a baseball bat. It hit my teeth. It really hurt!

Dentist: That was bad luck! I'll take a careful look. People sometimes ¹ ____________ their teeth in those kinds of accidents.

She examines Yudi's mouth.

Dentist: Good news, Yudi! The bat didn't do any damage. And none of your teeth have a ² ____________ , so you don't need a ³ ____________ . You can go back to the ⁴ ____________ now, and your mom can arrange your next ⁵ ____________ with the receptionist.

Yudi: Oh, that is good news! How often should I have checkups , Dr. Lee?

Dentist: An ⁶ ____________ checkup is fine. I'll see you next year, Yudi!

Yudi: Thank you, Dr. Lee. See you next year!

A **Match to make sentences with similes.**

1 The clouds were as fluffy as …   **a** excited kangaroos.

2 The surface of the lake was as smooth as …   **b** needles on my skin.

3 The children bounced down the street like …   **c** glass.

4 She ate quickly, like …   **d** baby lambs.

5 The freezing air felt like …   **e** a hungry bear.

B **Complete these similes with your own ideas.**

1 Snow covered the town like ______________________.

2 I felt as tired as ______________________.

3 The sand on the beach felt like ______________________ between my toes.

C **Write a paragraph to describe a visit to a place. Use similes with *as … as* and *like*.**

As I climbed the hill, I felt like a 90-year-old trying to run a marathon, and my breathing was as noisy as an excited dog's. But the view from the top of the hill was wonderful. I could see the whole city from up there. It looked like a blanket of little gray and brown squares, with bigger green patches where there were parks. The river cut through the middle of the city like a wiggling blue snake.

____

____

____

____

A **Unscramble the words to complete the paragraphs.**

1 I went to the dentist for my [1]a_____________ (nlanua) checkup last week. Checkups don't usually [2]s_____________ (carse) me. But when the dentist noticed that I had a [3]c_____________ (itcyva), I got a little worried. Luckily, it didn't hurt when he gave me a [4]f_____________ (lnigfli).

2 I love looking at the clouds. It's so [5]r_____________ (ignlarxe)! Fluffy, white clouds are very [6]c_____________ (mocomn) here, but last week I saw a very unusual cloud [7]f_____________ (atfromoni). It was [8]l_____________ (wol) in the sky, and it was a perfect circle shape.

B **Read and circle the correct option.**

The river in my town doesn't often [1]**entertain / oar / flood**, but last year it broke its banks. It was [2]**forever / terrifying / solid**! A lot of people were [3]**stranded / overboard / looked forward to** on the top floor of their homes. They were starting to [4]**entertain / run out of / chip** food when people in boats finally came to [5]**rescue / yacht / stuck** them.

C **Read and complete the dialogues. Use the correct form of *will* or *going to* and the verbs in parentheses.**

1 **A:** Do you have any plans for the weekend?
   B: Yes, I _____________________ (go) trampolining.

2 **A:** Why does she need eggs?
   B: She _____________________ (bake) a cake.

3 **A:** Can we go to the shopping mall this evening?
   B: OK. But the stores _____________________ (not be) open after 6:00 p.m.

4 **A:** Should I buy Sara this book?
   B: Good idea! I think she _____________________ (love) it.

5 **A:** No one on the team is very good at soccer.
   B: Yes, I can see that! They _____________________ (not win) the game.

Think and Reflect: Unit 5

My understanding of perspective ☆☆☆☆☆

How well I achieved my goal for Unit 5 ☆☆☆☆☆

The most interesting thing that I learned _____________________

My goal for Unit 6 _____________________

6 Why is it important to consider other people's perspectives?

Vocabulary 1

A Complete the sentences.

crowd   vote   residents   fancy   chime   thought

1 Does the clock in the town square ________________ every hour?

2 There's a big ________________ of people watching the street dancers.

3 The ________________ in my apartment building are very friendly.

4 I just had a really good ________________ .

5 Let's ________________ for our favorite book.

6 Our teacher wore a very ________________ hat last summer!

B Match to make sentences.

1 Many people feel concerned about …   a others think and feel.
2 Families gather for …   b if you play loud music.
3 Some people nod their head to show they …   c the plastic pollution in our oceans.
4 The neighbors will complain …   d on time.
5 When I have an appointment, I like to be …   e special days and events.
6 It's good to consider how …   f agree.

A **Complete the sentences with these nouns and the suffix -less.**

sleep   thought   tooth   ~~sugar~~   taste   rest   hope   end

1 Some people think that ___sugarless___ candies are ______________, but I don't agree. I think they're delicious!

2 I had a ______________ night. I kept moving around because I felt very ______________.

3 Gianni was ______________ when he didn't call his grandmother. She was upset.

4 We traveled across the mountains by bus. It was a long journey that seemed ______________.

5 At first, the rescuers thought the situation was ______________ but they found the hikers after a long search.

6 The tiger was so old that it was ______________ and couldn't eat properly.

B **Check (✓) the correct option.**

1 I'm meeting my friend on Sunday at ten o'clock.

  ☐ Prediction   ☐ Future arrangement

2 Our parents are bringing the trees and shovels to the garden at 9:30 a.m.

  ☐ Prediction   ☐ Future arrangement

3 It's already 30 degrees and it's only 9:00 a.m., so it's going to be a hot day.

  ☐ Future plan   ☐ Prediction

4 The sun will set at 6:00 p.m.

  ☐ Future fact   ☐ Future arrangement

5 We're all going to have dinner together when the trees are planted.

  ☐ Prediction   ☐ Future plan

6 We're going to help plant trees in the community garden.

  ☐ Future plan   ☐ Future fact

C **Complete each sentence with ONE word.**

1 I think my teacher ______________ help me understand this math puzzle.

2 We ______________ meeting at 8:30 a.m. at the teachers' room.

3 I need to leave soon because I ______________ seeing my teacher before class.

4 She's very smart, so I'm sure she ______________ have a problem understanding it.

5 There are big, black clouds in the sky. It's obviously ______________ to rain very soon.

6 I ______________ going to take a raincoat and an umbrella so I don't get wet.

D **Complete the sentences.**

1 ______________________________ start at 10:00 a.m.

2 ______________________________ set at 8:32 p.m. tonight.

3 ______________________________ a beautiful day.

4 ______________________________ her dentist for a checkup next week.

5 ______________________________ at the community center this afternoon.

6 ______________________________ take a lot of pictures when I go to the beach.

E **Unscramble the sentences.**

1 not / playing baseball / on / Saturday / We / are

____

2 my / I / seeing / cousins / later / am

____

3 going / this afternoon / have fun / We / are / to

____

4 a picnic / planning / are / We / the park / in

____

5 it / be / will / sunny today / think / I

____

F **Complete the sentences with the correct form of the verbs in parentheses.**

1 My family ______________________________ (move) to Canada on May 15. Mom has a new job and we've found an apartment.

2 Watch out! There's a big hole in the sidewalk. You ______________________________ (fall)!

3 Next June, I ______________________________ (be) twelve years old.

4 The spelling test ______________________________ (begin) at 9:00 a.m. so don't be late!

5 My aunt is looking forward to seeing her friends. She ______________________________ (travel) to Spain on Monday morning.

6 It ______________________________ (not / rain). The sky is blue and it's sunny.

A **Read the historical fiction story. What was wrong with the bats' home?**

Pietranova's Famous Bats

In 1923, fifty years after Pietranova's tower was built, as the sun began to set, the residents went to Piazza Galbani to watch a breathtaking display. They did this every evening. The tower of Pietranova was now famous throughout Italy for one special reason – a huge colony* of bats that called it home. Scientists from all over the world came to study the tiny animals, and tourists arrived daily to take pictures. The people of Pietranova loved the bats and were proud of them.

Then, one warm September evening, the people gathered as usual in Piazza Galbani, waiting for the bats to take flight. As the minutes ticked by, the crowd became concerned. Not a single bat left the tower.

"Maybe the bats didn't like our fancy Ferragosto* decorations last month." said Lucia, the town's oldest resident.

"I think you're right," said Mayor Mauro, nodding sadly, "It's fall now, so we should take them down."

"Or maybe …," said a young girl named Alessia, "there's something happening in the tower that we haven't considered." Several people turned to look at Alessia.

"The bats have all they need," complained a voice in the crowd. "They have shelter, a beautiful tower, clean air, and thousands of insects to eat! What more could they want?"

"Let's find out," replied Alessia as she walked toward the tower. Alessia, Mayor Mauro, and Lucia climbed the 99 steps of the tower quietly. When they finally reached the top, Lucia shone a torch on the tower's ceiling.

"That's the reason!" she announced. "Look! There's a hole in the roof! That big storm we had last week has made the bats' home dripping wet! No wonder they're unhappy."

It took just a few minutes for the crowd in Piazza Galbani to vote and agree to fix the roof immediately. A few weeks later, the people gathered once more at sunset. The mayor clapped his hands to attract attention.

"People of Pietranova! Let's rename this tower to celebrate its famous residents. Let's call it *Torre dei Pipistrelli* – the bats' tower. I'm meeting the painters tomorrow at ten. We'll make a new sign for the door!" The crowd cheered loudly, and as they cheered, the first bat came flying out of the tower, then another, and another until the red evening sky was filled with tiny happy bats dancing and circling.

Glossary:
colony = a group of animals, birds, insects of the same type that live together
Ferragosto = a public holiday in Italy celebrated on August 15

B **Underline these words in the text.**

gathered   complained   concerned   fancy   considered   vote   nodding

C **Read and circle *True* or *False*.**

1 In 1923, the town of Pietranova was famous because of its tourists.   **True**   **False**
2 Scientists were interested in the bat colony.   **True**   **False**
3 The people of Pietranova didn't care about the bats.   **True**   **False**
4 Lucia thought the bats didn't like the town's decorations.   **True**   **False**
5 The people voted to fix the tower.   **True**   **False**
6 The bats never returned to Pietranova's tower.   **True**   **False**

D **Answer the questions. If you need to, read the story again.**

1 Where does the story take place? Which town and country?

____

2 When is the story set? Is it in the present, past, or future?

____

3 What time of year or season is it when Alessia finds the hole in the roof?

____

4 What time of day does the story mention? Why is it important?

____

What are the people in your town or city proud of? Why?

A **Match to make sentences.**

1 Taking someone's TV from their house is a … •   • **a** permission.

2 People shouldn't take things without … •   • **b** fine.

3 If I say something unkind, I always … •   • **c** crime.

4 Drivers who go too fast can get a … •   • **d** guilty.

5 Piero took the money, so he's … •   • **e** jail.

6 People who do terrible things often go to … •   • **f** apologize.

B **Read and complete the paragraph.**   guilty   punishment   jail   accuses   crime

I'm reading a fantastic detective novel. It's set 50 years ago. The Gray Prince is a very powerful person and everyone is afraid of him. One day, the Gray Prince [1] _______________ his best friend, Octavius, of taking and selling his sports car without permission. He wants the police to send him to [2] _______________ immediately. Octavius says he isn't [3] _______________ of the [4] _______________, but he's scared of getting an unfair [5] _______________, so he runs away. I'm excited to find out what happens in the next chapter!

A Check (✓) the correct option.

1 Many people … me when I did the run.

☐ participated   ☐ sponsored

2 I have an …, so I can't eat eggs or nuts.

☐ allergy   ☐ sponsor

3 We live near this beautiful ….

☐ nature reserve   ☐ allergy

4 We're going to … for our school.

☐ involve   ☐ raise funds

5 It's fun to … your friends in outdoor activities.

☐ involve   ☐ participate

6 Many students at our school want to … in the school play.

☐ sponsor   ☐ participate

B Complete the sentences.

participate   raise   sponsor   nature reserve   involve   allergy

1 Last year, my best friend and I decided to ___________________ funds for new nest boxes in our local ___________________ to provide shelter for the birds.

2 We soon discovered that our families wanted us to ___________________ them, too, so we asked them to ___________________ in a bake sale.

3 My younger brother has a serious ___________________ to peanuts, so he didn't want to do any baking. He asked people to ___________________ him on a 10 kilometer bike ride instead.

A **Read the opinion essay. Label the different sections.**

Second paragraph   Conclusion   Opening statement and opinion

A New Downtown Area

In my opinion, the downtown part of our city should be made more attractive so that residents can spend time there relaxing and enjoying nature. Right now, there's a lot of pollution from cars and buses. I feel strongly that we need to reduce the pollution. We could achieve this quickly by turning downtown into an area for pedestrians only. There would be no traffic congestion and the city would be a lot quieter. In addition, city planners could arrange for people to plant trees. That will help clean up the air naturally.

We also need to consider how people want to use the area. At the moment, people go there to shop, visit cafés, and meet friends. The problem is that there's nowhere comfortable to sit and relax. My idea is to add some benches for people to sit on and tables where residents could eat lunch or play a game. Recycled materials can be used to make flower-planting boxes. We could also invite local artists to decorate the space with colorful paintings. The area would become a calm and friendly space for people of all ages to enjoy.

Finally, I think that a new pedestrian area would be great for the health of the city's residents. I saw a documentary that showed that people walk and exercise a lot more when they have a safe space far away from cars. That's really good for our mental and physical health! In my view, we should put the needs of people at the center of our downtown planning, not cars.

B **Check (✓) the correct option.**

1 Which part of the opinion essay states that comfort and color is needed downtown?

- ☐ opening statement and opinion
- ☐ second paragraph
- ☐ conclusion

2 Which part of the essay describes the benefit to people's well-being?

- ☐ opening statement and opinion
- ☐ second paragraph
- ☐ conclusion

C You're going to write an opinion essay. Brainstorm.
Write your ideas in the graphic organizer below.

D Do some research and outline your ideas by completing the chart.

Opinion:

Reason 1:

Reason 2:

Reason 3:

Reason 4:

Conclusion:

E Now write the first draft of your opinion essay in your notebook.

- Start with a statement that clearly gives your opinion.
- Use *in my opinion, I think that, in my view,* or *I feel/believe that* to write about your opinion.
- Organize your essay into paragraphs and give information that explains your opinion.
- In your conclusion, write a final sentence that restates your opinion.

F Check your work and make any necessary changes.

- Did you do everything in the list in **E**?
- Is your grammar, spelling, and punctuation correct?
- Is your writing clear and easy for other people to understand?

G Now write the final draft of your opinion essay in your notebook. 

A Read and circle the correct option.

Last weekend, I was at a concert in the park to [1]**apologize / raise funds** for the "Save the Whales" organization. I went with my family and we joined a huge [2]**crowd / gather** in the park. The music was so good that it made us stop and [3]**sponsor / consider** how lucky we were. We want to go to the nature [4]**appointment / reserve** next weekend. I hope it doesn't rain!

B Circle the correct answer.

1 What might make you complain?   **a** getting bad food in a café   **b** seeing your friends

2 What can you participate in?   **a** a book   **b** a game

3 What might you have an allergy to?   **a** nuts   **b** water

4 What might you get if you commit a crime?   **a** a fine   **b** a report

C Complete the sentences with the correct form of the verb.

	Future arrangements	**Future facts or predictions about things you believe**	**Future plans and predictions about things you see**
1 meet	I ____________ my grandma at the mall in an hour.	I think I ____________ a lot of interesting people when I'm older.	I ____________ some friends.
2 see	____________ we ____________ our teacher after class?	We ____________ the plane when it lands in 10 minutes.	____________ she ____________ her new puppy soon?
3 not start	They ____________ a new project next semester.	The astronauts ____________ the spaceship's engine today.	Uh-oh. The car ____________ .

Think and Reflect: Unit 6

My understanding of perspective ☆☆☆☆☆

How well I achieved my goal for Unit 6 ☆☆☆☆☆

The most interesting thing that I learned ____________________________________

My goal for Unit 7 ____________________________________

7 Where do we find beauty?

Vocabulary 1

A **Check (✓) the correct option.**

1 It's fascinating to see the … threads of a spider's web.

☐ delicate ☐ inspiration

2 Macrophotography is a … type of photography.

☐ sophisticated ☐ lens

3 The ocean will … the footprints in the sand.

☐ symmetry ☐ wash away

4 I … paintings, but I prefer looking at photographs.

☐ capture ☐ appreciate

5 Where did Claude Monet get his … from?

☐ inspiration ☐ masterpiece

6 There are some … pieces of art in the museum.

☐ reflection ☐ astonishing

7 My mom just took a photograph of the … sunset.

☐ stunning ☐ sophisticated

8 These paintings … the beauty of the small village.

☐ capture ☐ wash away

B **Match to make sentences.**

1 You can find a lens …
2 You might see a masterpiece …
3 You could capture …
4 You can see a stunning …
5 You can see a reflection …
6 You can get inspiration …
7 You can see symmetry …
8 You can show people you appreciate them …

a a fish in a fishing net.
b by thanking them when they help you.
c view from the top of the mountain.
d in a butterfly, a star, a face, and a leaf.
e in a camera.
f on the wall in an art gallery.
g at art museums.
h of yourself in the lake.

A **Read and circle the correct option.**

I read a very [1] **amused** / **amusing** story last week. It was so good that I was [2] **inspiring** / **inspired** to write a story of my own! Mine wasn't funny, but I tried to make it a little [3] **frightened** / **frightening**. The main character, Matilde, is [4] **confused** / **confusing** when she wakes up in a different country. Then, a wolf starts to follow her down the street! It's [5] **fascinated** / **fascinating** how easy it is to write a story when you have a good idea for a plot. My teacher was [6] **astonished** / **astonishing** when he read it. He said that it was much better than my other stories. In fact he said that it was [7] **amazing** / **amazed** and I should enter it in a writing contest. I felt [8] **embarrassing** / **embarrassed** at first because I don't like being the center of attention, but my classmates loved my story!

B **Are these sentences direct speech or reported speech? Read and check (✓).**

1 "Nature inspires me," said the painter.

☐ direct speech   ☐ reported speech

2 My sister said that she really enjoyed seeing the beach art.

☐ direct speech   ☐ reported speech

3 Our teacher said that Claude Monet was French.

☐ direct speech   ☐ reported speech

4 "I don't like street art," said Jay.

☐ direct speech   ☐ reported speech

C **Complete the reported speech.**

1 "I want to go to the new art gallery."

Aditi said that she _______________ to go to the new art gallery.

2 "I can't go with you."

Jayanti said that she _______________ go with Aditi.

3 "My friends are coming over."

Jayanti said that her friends _______________ over.

4 "I need to research some artists."

Aditi said that she _______________ to research some artists.

5 "I don't have time to go out."

Jayanti said that she _______________ time to go out.

6 "I'm writing a report on famous painters."

Aditi said that she _______________ a report on famous painters.

1 "I'm writing a text message."

a ☐ Mom said that she wrote a text message.

b ☐ Mom said that she was writing a text message.

2 "We can have pasta for dinner."

a ☐ Dad says that we have pasta for dinner.

b ☐ Dad said that we could have pasta for dinner.

3 "I don't want to go to bed!"

a ☐ My little sister said that she didn't want to go to bed.

b ☐ My little sister said that she don't want to go to bed.

4 "They need help to fix the bike."

a ☐ He said that they needed help to fix the bike.

b ☐ He said that they are needing help to fix the bike.

E **Unscramble the sentences.**

1 that / was / her project / enjoying / she / said

The artist __________________________ .

2 said / was / she / designing / that / a mural

She __________________________ .

3 she / often / that / said / in the park / painted

She __________________________ .

4 that / said / she / couldn't / in the rain / paint

She __________________________ .

F **Complete the sentences for each child. Then use reported speech to write what they said.**

1 ______________________________

____

2 ______________________________

____

3 ______________________________

____

4 ______________________________

____

What did your family member or friend say to you today?

A **Read the art webpage. What three things did the children celebrate in their art?**

"Our Beautiful Planet":
An Art Contest for Children

About the contest:

This year's theme was "Our Beautiful Planet." We invited children aged between 8 and 14 to create a piece of art that captured the beauty of our world. We received an astonishing number of entries from 43 different countries! Some were paintings, others were photographs, and we even had some models and sculptures.

Our contest judge, Janneke van Vuren, said that she appreciated the quality of this year's art.

> "These creative, caring children are an inspiration to us all."
>
> **Janneke van Vuren**

Announcing this year's winners in the Our Beautiful Planet Contest!

Winner: ages 7 – 9

Mai, Chiang Mai, Thailand

Mai sent us this beautiful drawing of a girl watering plants. She used crayons to shade the sky a rich, blue color. We liked the smile in the ocean – our world looks happy! We also liked the way Mai included images of the moon and other planets near Earth. Mai said that she wanted to show that trees, plants, and flowers are a big part of the beauty we see around us. Taking good care of them is important for our planet's well-being. Mai's picture is called "Our Garden World."

Winner: ages 10 – 12

Fridrik, Reykjavik, Iceland

Fridrik's model is titled "Amazing Animals." This stunning creation uses animals made from modeling clay to celebrate the diversity of animals on Earth. Notice how animals as large as lions, alligators, and giraffes are sharing the space with little animals like frogs and fish. We can also see lush green grass and bright blue water. But there is danger in this scene, too. There is only one of each type of animal. Through his art, Fridrik encourages us to protect our animals and their habitats.

Gabriel, Punta Arenas, Chile

This image of water allows us to see raindrops and reflections of light up close. Macro photography shows us the clear drops against bright blue construction paper. Since he took up photography as a hobby three years ago, Gabriel has taken many pictures of bugs and plants. Recently, he had the idea of photographing liquids. Gabriel said that he enjoyed trying different lenses on his camera. After taking many pictures, he got the result he wanted. About 71% of our planet is water, so this was a great choice of subject. Gabriel named his macro picture "Blue Drops on Our Beautiful, Blue Planet."

B **Underline these words in the text.**

captured   appreciated   reflections
inspiration   lenses   astonishing   stunning

C **Answer the questions.**

1 What did the judge say about the children who entered the contest?

____

2 What does Mai think is important for our planet's well-being?

____

3 What did Fridrik use to create his model?

____

4 How did Fridrik show danger in the scene?

____

5 Why was Gabriel's raindrops picture a good choice for the contest?

____

D ⚙ **Read again. Stop and clarify. Circle the correct answer.**

1 What did the contest judge appreciate?

  a the beauty of the world   **b** the quality of the art

2 In Mai's drawing, what has a smile?

  a our world   **b** the moon and planets

3 What does Fridrik's model celebrate?

  a the diversity of animals   **b** Earth

4 When did Gabriel start photographing liquids?

  a three years ago   **b** recently

A **Complete the sentences.**

graceful   cute   legally   spectacular   scenery
amount   rare   landscapes

1 I love deer. The way they move is so ______________ .

2 People can't ______________ hunt the animals in the nature reserve.

3 Did you see the ______________ sunset last night?

4 There's a large ______________ of traffic in London, New York, and Buenos Aires.

5 My cat is so ______________ when she chases her own tail.

6 The ______________ here is really beautiful. I could look at it all day.

7 We saw many different ______________ on our trip, from mountains to deserts.

8 My uncle collects ______________ books that are hard to find.

B **Check (✓) the correct option.**

1 Waterfalls can look really … .

☐ rare   ☐ spectacular

2 Joe is only nine, so he can't drive a car … .

☐ legally   ☐ graceful

3 Some species of animal are becoming … .

☐ rare   ☐ graceful

4 My baby sister's smile is very … .

☐ cute   ☐ amount

5 The tourists love the beauty of the … .

☐ spectacular   ☐ landscape

6 I need 200 grams of flour to make this recipe, but I don't have the right … .

☐ scenery   ☐ amount

A Check (✓) the correct option.

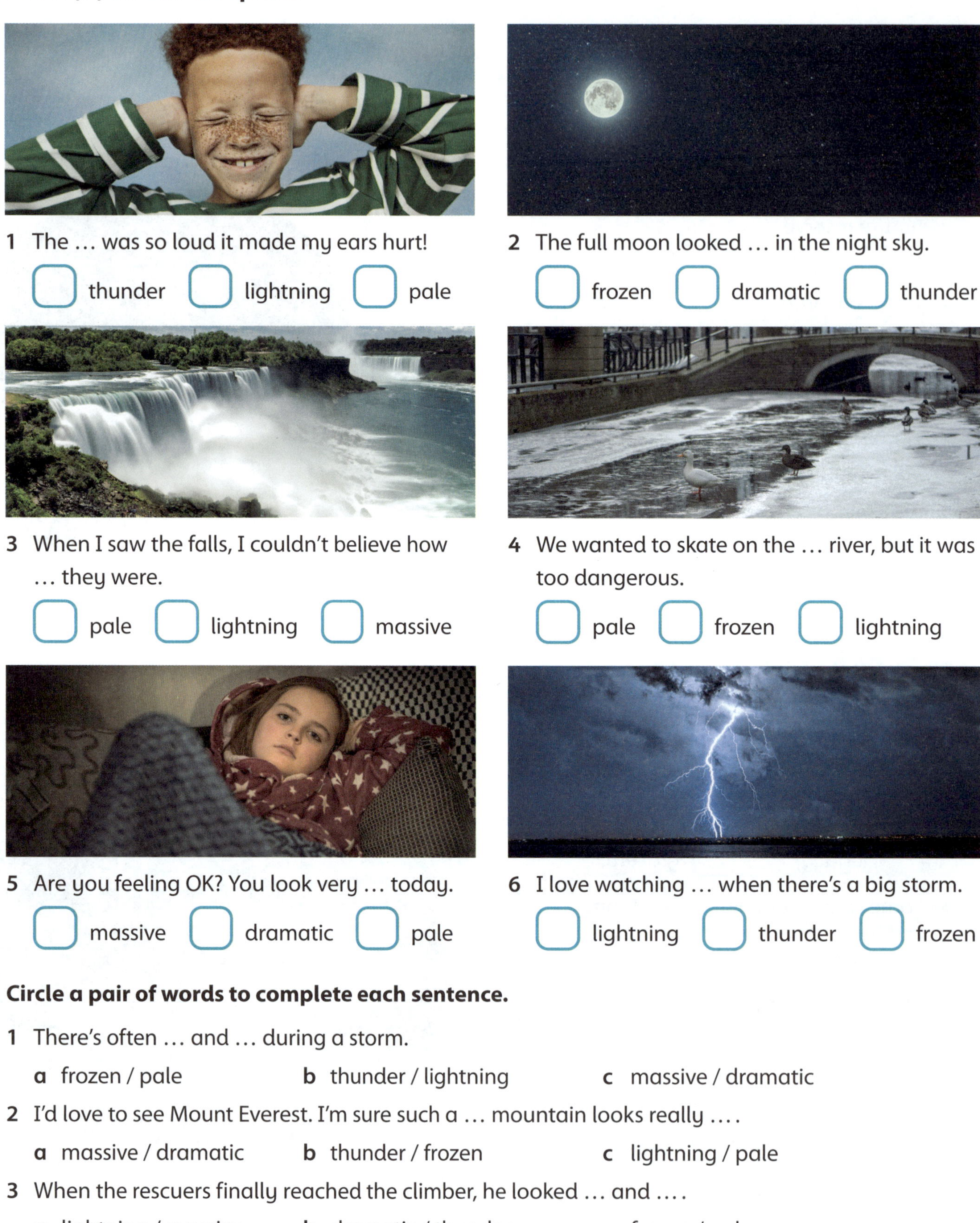

1 The … was so loud it made my ears hurt!

☐ thunder ☐ lightning ☐ pale

2 The full moon looked … in the night sky.

☐ frozen ☐ dramatic ☐ thunder

3 When I saw the falls, I couldn't believe how … they were.

☐ pale ☐ lightning ☐ massive

4 We wanted to skate on the … river, but it was too dangerous.

☐ pale ☐ frozen ☐ lightning

5 Are you feeling OK? You look very … today.

☐ massive ☐ dramatic ☐ pale

6 I love watching … when there's a big storm.

☐ lightning ☐ thunder ☐ frozen

B Circle a pair of words to complete each sentence.

1 There's often … and … during a storm.

  a frozen / pale   b thunder / lightning   c massive / dramatic

2 I'd love to see Mount Everest. I'm sure such a … mountain looks really ….

  a massive / dramatic   b thunder / frozen   c lightning / pale

3 When the rescuers finally reached the climber, he looked … and ….

  a lightning / massive   b dramatic / thunder   c frozen / pale

A Match the words with the definitions.

1 most
2 many
3 several

a a large number
b almost all, but not all
c more than two, but not a large number

B Complete the sentences with *most*, *many*, or *several*.

1 There are _________________ national parks in my country. I think there are four or five.

2 They legally protect _________________ of the animals that live in this park, but not the rabbits.

3 _________________ of the workers live inside the park. There are 20 workers and at least 16 live here.

4 _________________ of my friends live in my neighborhood. Only one of them lives in a different area.

5 I feel lucky because there are _________________ parks very close to where I live. I think there are three, maybe four.

6 _________________ residents agree that we should have a skateboard park in our community. When we voted, about 70% of my neighbors wanted one.

C Write a paragraph about your neighborhood. Use *most*, *many*, and *several*.

The town I live in is small but very interesting. Most of the buildings in my neighborhood are very old. Visitors like to take pictures of them. There are several stores, including a big supermarket and a computer store. Every week there's a farmers' market, too. Many people shop there. They like to buy fresh fruit and vegetables. Most of the sellers in the market are really friendly. I always wave and say hello when I see them. There isn't a park in my town, but there are several small community gardens. Every summer, my grandpa grows tomatoes in one of them.

____

____

____

____

A **Read and circle the correct option.**

Nature has been an [1] **inspiration / reflection / symmetry** to artists for hundreds of years. Painters and photographers love to [2] **wash away / capture / rare** the beauty of a [3] **thunder / lens / landscape** or the [4] **appreciate / symmetry / dramatic** they see in flowers. But you don't have to be an artist to [5] **amount / wash away / appreciate** the things around you. Who doesn't notice the [6] **dramatic / cute / frozen** power of a [7] **pale / lightning / delicate** storm or the [8] **stunning / sophisticated / masterpiece** sight of the sun rising?

B **Unscramble the words to complete the dialogue.**

A: I really [1] a______________ (createappi) nature. I love to watch the ocean [2] w______________ (shaw) a______________ (ayaw) footprints on the beach. I enjoy the [3] d______________ (atidramc) sight of the mountains. How about you?

B: I like the beauty of [4] f______________ (zenrof) water and the [5] p______________ (lape) color of the moon best of all. But I also love seeing [6] c______________ (tuec) baby rabbits with their [7] d______________ (licedtae) little ears and fluffy fur.

C **Find and cross out a mistake in each sentence with reported speech. Write the correct word.**

1 "I want to go to the beach."

My dad said that he want to go to the beach. ______________

2 "We can't go to the beach because it is too cold."

My mom said that we didn't go to the beach because it was too cold. ______________

3 "We can put a jacket on."

My sister said that we can put a jacket on. ______________

4 "We don't need jackets!"

Dad said that we didn't needed jackets. ______________

5 "I'm watching a movie."

I said that I'm watching a movie. ______________

Think and Reflect: Unit 7

My understanding of beauty ☆☆☆☆☆

How well I achieved my goal for Unit 7 ☆☆☆☆☆

The most interesting thing that I learned ______________________________________

My goal for Unit 8 ______________________________________

8 In what forms can we experience beauty?

A Read and match.

1 The water has gone.
2 She gave me a really expensive gift.
3 She wants a lot of money.
4 There's something wrong with her bike.
5 She loves that painting.

a She doesn't know how to repair it.
b Did it evaporate?
c She'll have to earn it.
d She thinks it's gorgeous.
e She's so generous.

B Read and circle the correct option.

Paolo sat down next to a beautiful [1] **magnificent / fountain** to [2] **juicy / gaze** at the ancient building. It looked [3] **magnificent / mouth-watering** against the blue sky. What a [4] **pleasure / tasty** it was to be there! After some time, he started to feel hungry, and he noticed a fruit seller nearby. Everything that she was selling looked very [5] **fountain / tasty**! There were [6] **pleasure / mouth-watering** cherries, melons, and grapes, but Paolo chose a peach. As he bit into it, orange liquid dripped from his mouth. It was [7] **gaze / juicy** and sweet – the perfect snack for this perfect day.

Word Study and Grammar

A Complete the sentences with these verbs.

> rewrite   retell   reheat   repay   rebuild   resend   reorganize   repaint

1 If you borrow money from a friend, it's important to _______________ it.

2 That was such a wonderful story! You should _______________ it to a bigger audience.

3 Your email didn't arrive. Could you _______________ it, please?

4 You're late for dinner, so your food's cold. You'll have to _______________ it on the stove.

5 It will take a long time to _______________ all the homes that the earthquake destroyed.

6 Can we _______________ my bedroom walls a different color?

7 I've decided to _______________ parts of my essay to make it clearer.

8 Let's _______________ the kitchen cabinets so everything is easier to find.

B What did Esma say? Complete the sentences.

	Direct Speech	Reported Speech
1	I never eat meat.	She told me that she never _______________ meat.
2	It's raining.	She told me that it _______________.
3	I can swim.	She told me that she _______________ swim.
4	Do you live here?	She asked me if I _______________ here.
5	What are you doing?	She asked me what I _______________.
6	Can you speak Turkish?	She asked me if I _______________ speak Turkish.

C Unscramble the words in parentheses to make reported questions.

1 Mom asked _______________________. (wanted / what / I / me)

2 I asked _______________________. (he / if / Sam / OK / was)

3 They asked _______________________. (were / you / running / you / why)

4 Our teacher asked _______________________. (us / help / if / could / we)

D Write what these people said in reported speech.

1 She told us _______________________ .

2 Arturo asked me _______________________ .

3 The article said _______________________ .

4 The server asked us if _______________________ .

E Correct the sentences.

1 She told they that she wanted to visit Barcelona.

____

2 We asked him why was he so happy.

____

3 He told us that he can juggle six balls!

____

4 They said me that they always loved staying with my aunt in Athens.

____

F Complete your speech bubbles. Then write what you said in reported speech.

I love _______________ .

I'm learning _______________ .

1 I told _______________ .

3 I said _______________ .

Do you want _______________ ?

When are you going _______________ ?

2 I asked _______________ .

4 I asked _______________ .

What is the nicest thing someone told you last week?

A **Read the travel blog. Which experience didn't Francisco enjoy? Why?**

Francisco's FOOD BLOG

About | Places | Explore | Tips

Hi, everyone! I've just finished my first year studying food science at college, and I got some fantastic news: I came top of my year! There's a generous prize for that. I'm going to use the prize money plus the money that I've earned from my evening job at a restaurant to go traveling this summer. Vietnam, here I come!

Ho Chi Minh City, Vietnam   June 26

I feel so lucky to be in this wonderful city. I've seen some stunning buildings today, and enjoyed a magnificent view from the top of the Bitexco Financial Tower. This evening, I asked some other travelers what they recommended for dinner. They told me I could find amazing street food on Cô Giang Street. As I walked along this incredible street, the sounds of soups bubbling and meats sizzling in oil surrounded me, and a mouth-watering smell hung in the air. I tried a lot of delicious snacks, but my favorite was *gỏi cuốn* – a little roll made from rice paper, with meat and salad inside. Gorgeous!

Ngã Năm, Vietnam   June 28

I got up at 4:00 a.m. this morning to go to a floating market. It was awesome! There were hundreds of boats on the Mekong River, selling fruit, vegetables, fresh flowers, and even live animals. I bought a mango, and it was the tastiest, juiciest fruit ever. All the food at the market comes from local farms in the Mekong valley, so it's extremely fresh.

While I was at the market, I met a friendly farmer named Hiep. He asked if I wanted to stay at his family's farmstay*. I told him that sounded like a great idea, so that's my plan for tomorrow!

Hiep's farm, Vietnam   July 1

I've been helping Hiep with the farm work. It's hot and tiring and not much fun – I prefer working in restaurants! But I've been enjoying learning some words in Vietnamese from Hiep's children. It's a beautiful language.

Earlier, we went out in their boat to look for something for dinner. We caught some shrimp and we also found a wetland plant named *bồn bồn*. I helped Hiep to peel the shrimps' hard, rough shells. Then his wife, Lim, cooked them in oil, with some onion and our bồn bồn stems. With noodles, this made a delicious meal.

Glossary:
farmstay = a farm where tourists can stay

B **Underline these words in the text.**

gorgeous   earned   magnificent   mouth-watering   tastiest   juiciest

C **Answer the questions.**

1 How did Francisco pay for his trip to Vietnam?

____

2 Did Francisco eat in a restaurant in Ho Chi Minh City? Why? / Why not?

____

3 Where do people sell things in Ngã Năm?

____

4 What's special about the fruit at the market in Ngã Năm?

____

5 How did Francisco learn some Vietnamese?

____

6 What did Francisco do to help with the dinner?

____

D **Find an example of descriptive language in the text that appeals to each of these senses.**

1 sight _______________________   4 taste _______________________

2 sound _______________________   5 touch _______________________

3 smell _______________________

A Read and circle the correct option.

What kind of music do you like? Some people enjoy a gentle, relaxing [1] **tune / heartbeat** on a recorder; others prefer something with a strong, [2] **expressive / rhythmic** drum beat that makes them want to dance. Some people prefer the [3] **steady / familiar** music that they've known for years; other people's musical interests [4] **last / tune** only a short time, as they keep discovering new favorites. Although people have very different tastes in music, almost all humans enjoy this [5] **repetitive / expressive** art form which can communicate emotion so well without the use of words.

B Complete the sentences.

> tune   steady   repetitive   expressive   heartbeat   familiar

1 Don't play more slowly when the music gets more difficult. Keep a _______________ rhythm!

2 Try to be more _______________ as you sing this song. Make it sound really sad!

3 Did you know that a hummingbird's _______________ is 150 times faster than a blue whale's?

4 I'm sure I recognize this music! It sounds very _______________ .

5 This song is boring and _______________ . It uses the same six words again and again.

6 This _______________ is gorgeous. It gives me so much pleasure every time I listen to it.

What kind of music do you like or dislike? Why?

A **Check (✓) the correct option.**

1 The audience's … filled the theater as they watched the funny movie.

   ☐ laughter   ☐ kindness

2 You look very … in your new coat.

   ☐ elegant   ☐ attached

3 It's an … town, with some magnificent old buildings and beautiful parks.

   ☐ attached   ☐ attractive

4 Thank you so much for your … .

   ☐ lamppost   ☐ kindness

5 If you're looking at a smartphone while you're walking on a sidewalk, you might walk into a … .

   ☐ lamppost   ☐ laughter

6 The note is … to the chair with tape.

   ☐ attractive   ☐ attached

B **Answer the questions.**

1 Why is there sometimes laughter in your class?

____

2 What parts of your body are attached to your hands?

____

3 What animals do you think are elegant?

____

4 How can you show kindness to your friends?

____

5 What's the most attractive building in your country?

____

6 Why are lampposts useful?

____

A Underline the option that won't work in the same parallel structure.

1 like dancing	like writing	like to sing
2 some butter	cut up the carrot	two onions
3 sit on the floor	lie in bed	a comfortable chair
4 go surfing	trampolining	basketball
5 afternoons	at night	in the morning

B Rewrite these sentences using a parallel structure.

1 Jose likes to sing, and he likes playing the flute, and writing songs.

Jose likes to sing, to play the flute, and to write songs.

2 My village has a restaurant, a sports club, and it has a grocery store.

3 For this recipe, you need sugar and flour and you need eggs.

4 On weekends, we enjoy drawing pictures, going to the movie theater, and to play soccer.

5 I gazed at the magnificent buildings, the gorgeous gardens, and beautiful fountains.

6 He ran across the field, over the bridge, and he ran up the hill.

C Write a paragraph about how you experience beauty in your life.

I enjoy seeing the attractive things around me. I sometimes photograph colorful butterflies, stunning landscapes, and elegant architecture. Then I put the photos on my bedroom walls, so I can appreciate their beauty when I'm lying in bed, when I'm getting ready for school, and when I'm doing my homework. I also love listening to beautiful music. I listen in the shower, in the car, and in my bedroom. Music is very important to me. Finally, I try to notice all the beautiful smells in my life: a cup of hot chocolate, a flowering plant, or my grandma's perfume.

A **Read and write *a*, *b*, or *c*.**

1 The fruit in that bowl looks ______ ! I'd love a ______ orange right now.

   a juicy　　　　　　**b** mouth-watering　　　　　　**c** generous

2 He has a ______ heartbeat, and he's feeling better. I don't think his stay in hospital will ______ long.

   a tune　　　　　　**b** last　　　　　　**c** steady

3 There's a pocket ______ to my jacket, but it's starting to fall off. Please could you help me to ______ it?

   a repair　　　　　　**b** attached　　　　　　**c** kindness

4 The river doesn't look very ______ in the summer. All the water has ______ so the river is dry.

   a gazed　　　　　　**b** attractive　　　　　　**c** evaporated

B **Unscramble the words to complete the paragraph.**

In ballet, we have to do the same slow, [1] r______________ (hrmythci) moves many times, but I don't mind those [2] r______________ (eritpevtie) exercises. I get a lot of [3] p______________ (uerpalse) from ballet because it's so [4] e______________ (repxisevse).

C **Write the reported speech.**

1 "I'm baking cookies!" said Dad.

   ____

2 "They smell gorgeous!" I told him.

   ____

3 "Do you want a cookie?" Dad asked me.

   ____

4 "You can have one after dinner," he told me.

   ____

5 "What is your favorite cookie flavor?" I asked him.

   ____

Think and Reflect: Unit 8

My understanding of beauty ☆☆☆☆☆

How well I achieved my goal for Unit 8 ☆☆☆☆☆

The most interesting thing that I learned ______________________________________

My goal for Unit 9 ____

9 Why does beauty matter?

A Circle the correct option.

1 The train is **plain** / **due** to arrive at 10:32 a.m.

2 People who play sports often get **dirt** / **silence** on their clothes.

3 This robot vacuum cleaner is good at cleaning **crate** / **dusty** floors.

4 This **crate** / **nightmare** is full of fresh vegetables.

5 This building is very **plain** / **dirt**.

6 These children look **confused** / **cheerful**.

B Read and complete the paragraph.

> silence   weed   confused   stare   dirt   ruined   dusty   nightmare

This morning I woke up feeling ¹_____________ by a ²_____________ I had while I was asleep. I don't often have bad dreams, but last night, I dreamed I was in the town center in a very ³_____________ street. My town is usually neat and clean, but there was ⁴_____________ everywhere. Every building I saw was ⁵_____________. It was so surprising that all I could do was ⁶_____________ at the place! No one was there and all I heard was ⁷_____________. Next, I bent down to pick a flower, but when I looked at it, it was a ⁸_____________, not a flower!

What dreams do you remember?

A **Complete the sentences with an adjective, adding *im-*, *in-*, or *un-* to make it negative.**

> polite   healthy   expensive   possible   safe
> attractive   correct   comprehensible

1 We went to a yard sale on the weekend. I bought several cool hats for $2. They were _______________.

2 Sven said New York was the capital of the U.S.A. That's _______________. The capital is Washington, D.C.

3 Eating a lot of fast food and candy is _______________. It's better to eat fruit and vegetables.

4 I'd love to be able to fly like a bird. It would be fun, but I know it's _______________.

5 I can't speak or understand Portuguese. This Portuguese TV show is _______________ to me.

6 Don't go over that bridge. It's very old and it looks _______________. It could fall down.

7 Tania never says "Thank you" for anything. It's very _______________.

8 There's a lot of trash in the city center. It makes the place look _______________.

B **Circle the correct option.**

Ahmed: Hello, Mia.

Mia: Hi, Ahmed! Where [1] **did you go** / **you went** last night?

Ahmed: I went to the school play. I really enjoyed it!

Mia: Cool! Who [2] **wrote** / **did write** the play?

Ahmed: One of the sixth-grade students wrote it. The costumes were great!

Mia: Who [3] **did make** / **made** the costumes?

Ahmed: Sonia made them. But there was a problem with the lion costume.

Mia: Why? What [4] **happened** / **did happen** to the lion costume?

Ahmed: It didn't have any ears!

C **Read the answers. Write the questions.**

1 **A:** ___________________________________ (where / go)

   B: We went to Finland.

2 **A:** ___________________________________ (who / go with)

   B: I went with my family.

3 **A:** ___________________________________ (what / happen)

   B: We watched movies on the plane.

4 **A:** ___________________________________ (where / eat)

   B: We ate at local restaurants.

5 **A:** ___________________________________ (who / choose)

   B: My mom chose the hotel.

D **Read and write *S* (Subject question) or *O* (Object question).**

1 What's in the box? ______

2 Where do anteaters live? ______

3 When does the store open? ______

4 Who cooked dinner? ______

5 What did you do yesterday? ______

6 What happened last night? ______

E **Imagine a friend or family member just returned from a vacation. Write questions you might want to ask them. Write two subject questions and two object questions.**

1 ____

2 ____

3 ____

4 ____

A **Read the fantasy story. How does Rafa's opinion of his grandmother's story change?**

A World of Color

Every year, Rafa's grandma told him the story about an event she experienced several times as a child. After a big rainstorm, everything that was gray, white, and black in their town turned into bright, happy colors. The strange thing was that no one ever knew when this might happen. Rafa smiled at his grandma. It was a nice story, but he didn't think it was true.

As Rafa walked to school early one morning, he was caught in a rainstorm. His uniform, shoes, and backpack all got soaked. For a moment, he felt annoyed, but then the warmth of the sun changed his attitude. *Springtime!* he thought, happily.

At that moment, a triple rainbow appeared! Rafa stopped and stared in surprise. At first, he was confused. He thought that triple rainbows were very rare! Next, a window opened, and hundreds of birds of all shapes and sizes flew out. These were not real birds – they were paper birds, beautifully made from delicate sheets of colored paper. Rafa was overjoyed at the sight.

Rafa turned into the main square. The plain, dusty gray buildings were now painted red, yellow, green, orange, and blue! *What's going on?* he wondered. The town hall was decorated with a million colorful flowers! In front of the town hall, there were huge crates of oranges, apples, strawberries, bananas, and pears!

Rafa's surprise turned to amazement when a crowd of cheerful people dressed in colorful clothes came dancing into the square. Some were banging drums and playing tunes on flutes, others were throwing colored water and flour into the streets. Rafa ran excitedly to the center of the square. As he ran, his school uniform turned from gray to yellow and purple. Even his hair, which was brown, turned pink! *All these years, Grandma was telling me a true story*, thought Rafa.

Rafa skipped into the park. Every tree, every bench, every trash can, every bird and animal was a different color. Rafa couldn't believe his eyes. A beautiful blue squirrel stopped on a green tree branch. It held a small orange weed. The squirrel seemed to smile at Rafa, and then disappeared.

As the sun set over the town, the colors faded and life returned to normal.

From this day on, thought Rafa as he fell asleep that night, *I'm going to do all I can to make the world a more colorful, happy place.*

B **Underline these words in the text.**

> dusty   confused   crates   weed   plain   cheerful   stared

C **Circle the correct option.**

1 At the beginning of the story, Rafa thought his grandma was telling him a **true** / **false** story.
2 After the **rainstorm** / **snowstorm**, Rafa saw a triple rainbow.
3 When a window opened, Rafa saw paper **flowers** / **birds** in the sky.
4 In the square, people were **throwing** / **drinking** colored water.
5 As Rafa ran threw the square, his uniform turned **gray** / **yellow and purple**.
6 In the park, Rafa noticed a blue **squirrel** / **tree**.

D ⚙ **Re-read the story. Find adjectives or sentences in the story that describe Rafa's feelings and attitudes. Complete the chart.**

	How did Rafa feel?	Why?
1		
2		
3		
4		
5		
6		

What stories did your parents or grandparents tell you?

A **Check (✓) the correct option.**

1 My grandmother doesn't enjoy shopping in the mall. It's too … .

☐ statistic   ☐ crowded

2 The doctor gave me … when I had an earache. It made me feel better.

☐ medication   ☐ infection

3 If you cut your finger, wash it quickly so you don't get an … .

☐ analyze   ☐ infection

4 The nurses work on a … in the hospital.

☐ statistic   ☐ ward

5 Jeanne had an … , but after a few days she was fine.

☐ illness   ☐ medication

6 Jon is unwell. I hope he can … quickly.

☐ analyze   ☐ recover

B **Read and complete the paragraph.**

statistics   analyzed   infection   ward   crowded   medication   recover

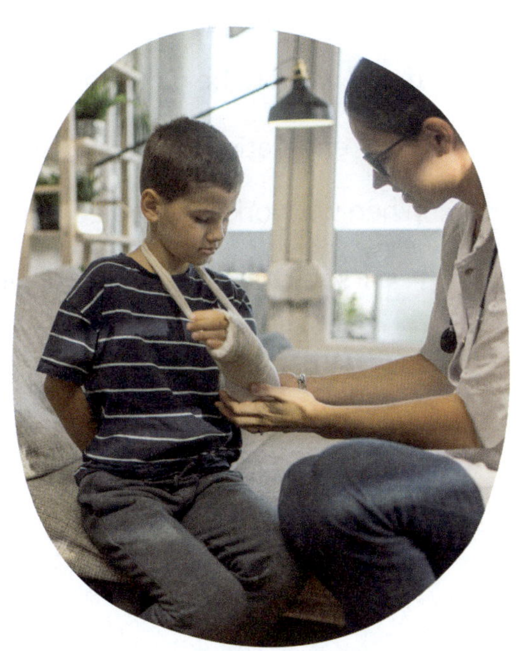

About a week ago, I was shopping with my family in the town center. It was very ¹ ________________ .
There were so many people! I wasn't watching where I was going and I fell over. I hurt my hand and broke my arm. My mom and dad took me to the hopital. The doctors ² ________________ the pictures of my arm.
They said that it was badly broken in two places, so for a few nights I stayed on a ³ ________________
for people with broken bones. The doctors gave me ⁴ ________________ because they didn't want me to get an ⁵ ________________ . They said that I was lucky because I can ⁶ ________________ quickly.
Next time I go into town, I'm going to be more careful.
⁷ ________________ show that the arm is one of the most common places in your body to break a bone!

A **Complete the sentences.**

zone   select   energetic   focused   comfortable   collaborate

1 There are so many movies to watch, but I don't know which one to ______________.

2 I don't enjoy working alone, so let's ______________.

3 I play many different sports because I'm very ______________.

4 I like the library because it has a quiet ______________.

5 Listening to music helps me to get ______________.

6 I love my bedrooom because it's very ______________.

B **Check (✓) the correct option.**

1 It's important to … shoes that are the right size for you.

☐ zone   ☐ select

2 When you have a difficult math problem to do, you need to be ….

☐ focused   ☐ energetic

3 Some trains have a quiet … where you can't use a smartphone or play music.

☐ zone   ☐ comfortable

4 Beds, chairs, and couches should all be ….

☐ energetic   ☐ comfortable

5 If you want to be a dancer, you need to be ….

☐ energetic   ☐ select

6 When we work on a project together, we ….

☐ select   ☐ collaborate

A **Read the travel guide. Label the different sections.**

First attraction   Last attraction   Third attraction
Welcoming message   Second attraction

Costa Rica – A Beautiful Country!

____

Come and visit Costa Rica! Costa Rica is famous for many things, including its stunning natural landscapes and national parks, its wildlife, its cool activities, and its delicious food.

____

First, let's begin with wildlife. Here in Costa Rica, you can go whale-watching in many places, including in some of the national parks, such as Corcovado National Park. Maybe you'll even see baby whales swimming in the calm waters. There are two seasons for whale-watching: December through March and July through October. Book your tour and jump on a boat. You won't be disappointed!

____

Next, we recommend a hike to the most beautiful waterfalls in Costa Rica – the Nauyaca Waterfalls. They're about 60 meters high! You can hike four kilometers through the rainforest and swim in the cool, blue water when you get there. If you don't like hiking, you can reach the falls on horseback or in a truck.

____

Then, how about exploring a cloud forest? These rare tropical forests sit under a blanket of mist and fog. We recommend going to the Children's Eternal Rainforest. Here, you'll see snakes, toucans, jaguars, sloths, and monkeys. It's also less crowded than other nature reserves.

____

Finally, don't forget to try some of the delicious food in Costa Rica. It's fresh, healthy, and not too spicy. Costa Rican people eat a lot of vegetables and fruit, as well as meat and fish. We love gallo pinto (rice and beans) and also the sweet fruit named guanabana. You can try both of these tasty things in the farmers' markets around the country.

Book your ticket to visit this wonderful country now!

B **Answer the questions.**

1 At the beginning of the travel guide, how does the writer introduce Costa Rica?

____

2 How does the writer present Costa Rica's attractions?

____

3 What details does the writer include in the travel guide?

____

C **You're going to write a travel guide. Brainstorm.
Write your ideas in the graphic organizer below.**

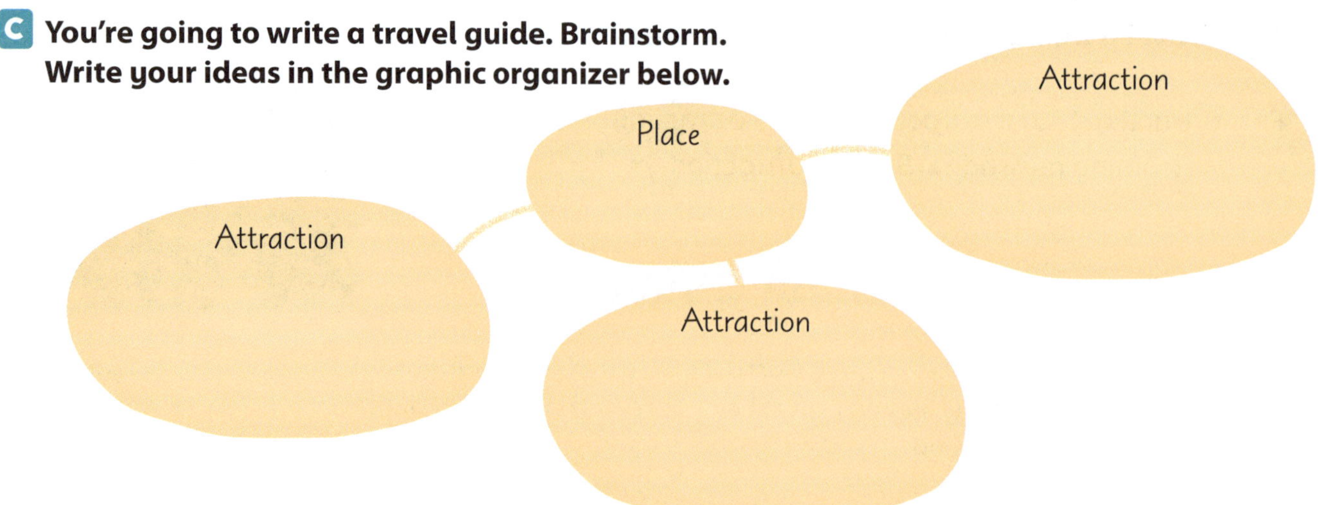

D **Do some research and plan your travel guide by completing the chart.**

Place:

Welcoming message:

Attraction 1:

Attraction 2:

Attraction 3:

Conclusion:

E **Now write the first draft of your travel guide in your notebook.** 

- Start your guide with a welcoming message that makes people want to visit.
- Include three interesting attractions or things to see and do in the country you chose.
- Use transition words (*first, next, then, finally*) to organize what you want to say.
- Write a concluding sentence.

F **Check your work and make any necessary changes.**

- Did you do everything in the list in **E**?
- Is your grammar, spelling, and punctuation correct?
- Is your writing clear and easy for other people to understand?

G **Now write the final draft of your travel guide in your notebook.**

Unit Review

A **Unscramble the words to complete the dialogues.**

1 **A:** What's wrong? You're usually so ¹ c______________ (clufeerh), but you aren't very happy today.

 B: Last night, I had a ² n______________ (nregtmaih). It was scary. I dreamed I was in a ³ c______________ (cworded) room. It was dirty and ⁴ d______________ (dtysu).

2 **A:** I think I've caught an ⁵ i______________ (issenll). Usually I feel ⁶ f______________ (fcusedo) and ⁷ e______________ (egetnicer), but I feel awful today.

 B: You should see a doctor. You might need ⁸ m______________ (mcatdinoei) to ⁹ r______________ (rveecor).

B **Complete the sentences.**

> due   comfortable   zone   select

1 Some trains have a quiet ______________ . You're not allowed to make calls or play music.

2 The living room in my house has three ______________ chairs to sit on.

3 To complete this puzzle, I need to ______________ the correct words.

4 Do you know when the Number 6 bus is ______________ ?

C **Read the answers. Complete the questions.**

1 **A:** What ______________ in the sky?
 B: He saw some clouds.

2 **A:** Who ______________ to school with him?
 B: Peter goes to school with him.

3 **A:** Who ______________ that skateboard?
 B: His mom bought that skateboard.

4 **A:** Who ______________ those sandwiches?
 B: His dad made those sandwiches.

5 **A:** Where ______________ ?
 B: He went to the park.

6 **A:** When ______________ ?
 B: The train leaves at 6 o'clock.

Think and Reflect: Unit 9

My understanding of beauty ☆☆☆☆☆

How well I achieved my goal for Unit 9 ☆☆☆☆☆

The most interesting thing that I learned ______________________________

My goal for Unit 10 ______________________________

10 What can we do to acquire knowledge?

Vocabulary 1

A Complete the sentences.

give up   bend   safety   copy   join in   trick

1 The firefighter is wearing ________________ equipment.

2 This is a skateboarding ________________ I learned last week.

3 Sometimes I ________________ everything that my dad does!

4 Even when things are hard, I never ________________ .

5 I like to ________________ with my friends when they're playing games.

6 It's pretty difficult to ________________ your back!

B Circle the correct option.

1 I love dancing. I learned two new **feedback** / **moves** today.

2 My teacher gave me a good **tip** / **basic** for remembering new words.

3 Sometimes we give our classmates **feedback** / **safety** in class.

4 Have you seen this movie? It has great **tips** / **reviews**.

5 The actors on this TV show are **feedback** / **well known**.

6 I'd like to find some **basic** / **review** facts about lions.

A Complete the sentences with the correct phrasal verb. Use a word from each box.

hand   fall   look   write   cross   stand

up   down   up   out   off   out

1 Let's ___________________ the questions.

2 Everyone please ___________________!

3 Now I'm going to ___________________ your books.

4 I don't know this word. I'm going to ___________ it ___________.

5 That's wrong. I'll ___________ it ___________.

6 Look out! Don't ___________ the ladder.

B Complete the chart.

	Question	Short Yes Answer	Short No Answer
1	Are you …?	Yes, I am.	No, I'm not.
2	Does he …?		No, he doesn't.
3	Can you …?	Yes, I can.	
4	Do they …?		No, they don't.
5	Was he …?	Yes, he was.	
6	Were we …?		No, we weren't.
7	Could she …?	Yes, she could.	
8	Will they …?	Yes, they will.	
9	Did they …?		No, they didn't.
10	Has he …?	Yes, he has.	

Which of the actions in A have you done today?

C Read the questions. Complete the short answers.

1 Can you speak Arabic? No, I _________________ .

2 Did Mike and Misha pass the quiz? Yes, they _________________ .

3 Will we have hot weather this summer? Yes, we _________________ .

4 Are they going to buy new T-shirts? Yes, they _________________ .

5 You could ride a bike when you were three, couldn't you? No, I _________________ .

6 You've seen a snake before, haven't you? Yes, I _________________ .

D Look and write answers to the questions.

1 Can she drive a fire truck?

____

2 Are they sad?

____

3 Did she win the bike race?

____

4 They were studying last night, weren't they?

____

5 Will he go swimming this weekend?

____

6 She's wearing a baseball cap, isn't she?

____

E Answer the questions so they're true for you. Use short answers.

1 Can you play a musical instrument?   _________________

2 You like watching scary movies, don't you?   _________________

3 Did you study biology last year?   _________________

4 Will you be an adult next year?   _________________

5 Were you shy when you were very young?   _________________

6 You could swim when you were two years old, couldn't you?   _________________

A **Read the magazine interview. Apart from math, what did Joaquin learn from entering the competition?**

Joaquin Rodriguez Math Fan

Today, we're interviewing a 13-year-old math fan, Joaquin Rodriguez. Joaquin has just won this year's International Math Olympiad competition.

Math Buddies: Joaquin, you just scored very highly in this incredibly hard competition. How do you feel?

Joaquin: I feel proud of myself, I guess. It was *hard*!

Math Buddies: Why did you enter the competition?

Joaquin: I like solving real problems. This year, one of the problems was about future weather patterns. The solutions could help farmers plan better, and I think that's cool.

Math Buddies: It *is* cool! Tell us a little more about the competition. Who can enter?

Joaquin: To enter you have to be under 20 years old. There are six problems to solve and you're not allowed to use a calculator!

Math Buddies: How did you first get interested in math?

Joaquin: I got interested in basic math when I was around five years old. Mom took me to some really great science museums and there were all kinds of puzzles for children. Then a little later, my first grade math teacher encouraged me a lot.

Math Buddies: What methods did you use to improve?

Joaquin: When people noticed that I liked math, they started giving me math books! By the time I was seven, I had a big collection of books. I used them every day.

Math Buddies: Did technology help you?

Joaquin: Yes, it did! When I was about ten, I started watching math videos to learn how to figure things out. A year later, I used many websites that are well known and offer free math practice.

Math Buddies: That's cool. But isn't it lonely just doing math on your own?

Joaquin: I'm not always alone. Last year I joined several math clubs, both online and in my neighborhood. They're a great way to get useful feedback and tips from people who are better at math than you are. Everyone joins in to solve math problems together. It's a lot of fun!

Math Buddies: Was the competition scary? I heard the problems are really, really hard to get right!

Joaquin: Yes, it was scary, but I learned a lot, not just about math, but about me.

Math Buddies: Oh? What do you mean?

Joaquin: I learned that if you want to do something, you should never give up, even when it's really hard.

Math Buddies: That's an important lesson to learn! And what's next for you?

Joaquin: I want to learn to cook! Math is great, but so is tasty food!

Math Buddies: That's great! I'm sure you'll be fantastic at it. Thanks for talking to us today.

B Underline these words in the text.

> feedback   well known   basic   tips   joins in   give up

C Read and write *True* or *False*.

1 To enter the International Math Olympiad competition, you have to be 13. ___________

2 You can't use a calculator to solve the problems in the competition. ___________

3 Joaquin didn't like using technology. ___________

4 Joaquin only belongs to online math clubs. ___________

5 Joaquin thought the competition was scary. ___________

6 Joaquin can already cook really well. ___________

D Think about Joaquin's journey to winning the competition. Number the steps in order.

1	2	3	4	5

beginner   **champion**

a ☐ He joined math clubs online and in his neighborhood.

b ☐ He went to science museums with his mom.

c ☐ He watched math videos online.

d ☐ He used math websites to practice.

e ☐ He used a big collection of math practice books.

f ☐ His first grade teacher encouraged him.

A **Read and complete the dialogue.**

ban   savory   stink   dare   mix   announce   edible

Ella: I'm bored of waiting in the airport.
What time are we going to get on the plane?

Jack: I'm not sure. Maybe they'll [1] ______________ it soon.

Ella: Can I take these peanuts on board?

Jack: No, you can't. Airlines [2] ______________ nuts because some people have allergies.

Ella: Oh, right. I'll take these [3] ______________ chips then. They're a delicious
[4] ______________ of cheese and onion. Mmmm!

Jack: Please don't. They smell terrible. I think they [5] ______________!

Ella: No, they don't! They're yummy. I [6] ______________ you to try one. Come on!

Jack: No, thank you. They don't even look [7] ______________ to me! Take an apple instead.

B **Complete the sentences.**

spike   edible   savory   mix   ban   stink

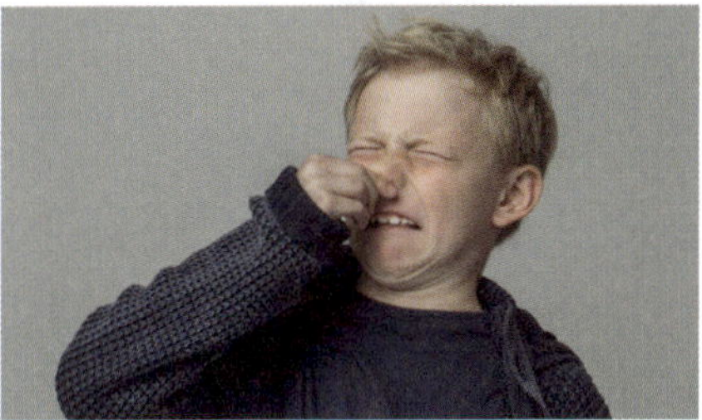

1 Sometimes, some things ______________!

2 These foods all taste ______________, not sweet.

3 This insect has a long ______________ on its head.

4 Buses and trains often ______________ passengers from eating food on board.

5 I made this cake with a ______________ of flour, eggs, sugar, and butter.

6 Don't eat this mushroom. I'm sure it's not ______________.

A **Read and circle *True* or *False*. Correct the false sentences.**

1 Fruit can be dried.

True   False

____

2 A greenhouse is a place animals live in.

True   False

____

3 An example of a figure is 3,000.

True   False

____

4 A teacher is a person who's in charge of a class.

True   False

____

5 If you have up-to-date information, it's old and not very useful.

True   False

____

6 A reliable friend is someone who promises to do something but forgets.

True   False

____

B **Complete the sentences.**

reliable   up-to-date   greenhouse   figures   dried   in charge of

1 I'm often _______________ my little brother, so I play with him a lot.

2 I wear _______________ clothes, so I look fashionable.

3 I like _______________ fruit, so I'll try these apple slices.

4 I want _______________ information, so I go to the school library.

5 I don't have a _______________ , so I can't grow plants in the winter.

6 I like working with _______________ , so I enjoy my math classes.

A **Write sentences using the prompts and the words in parentheses. Don't forget to use commas.**

1 I like many healthy snacks / carrots, apples, and nuts. (such as)

2 I went to some interesting places in Mexico / Puebla, Izamal, and Yelapa. (for example)

3 My best friend plays a lot of sports / baseball, judo, and soccer. (for instance)

B **Read the sentences. Rewrite them as one sentence. Use *for instance, for example,* or *such as,* and commas.**

1 There are a lot of music classes in my school. There are classes for piano, guitar, and violin.

2 I belong to many different clubs. I belong to clubs for coding, dance, and drama.

3 I enjoy several types of movies. I enjoy action, adventure, and sci-fi movies.

C **Write a paragraph to describe the things you did or learned this month. Use *for instance, for example, such as,* and commas.**

This month I learned a lot about knowledge in class. I learned about the ways people acquire knowledge, such as how to skateboard, how to choose safety equipment, and how to get feedback. I also learned about some skateboarding tricks, for instance, an ollie and a drop-in! After that, I found out about unusual fruits, for example, the durian. That was funny because I discovered that it stinks, but it tastes delicious!

A Unscramble the words to complete the paragraphs.

1 I joined a breakdancing club this month. Now I know some really cool [1] m_____________ (soevm). The teacher taught us a lot of [2] t_____________ (kscirt) you can do to make it look like you're almost flying! We took turns to perform and then gave each other [3] f_____________ (eebdfkca). It was fun!

2 My little brother Kit decided to do some cooking. Mom watched. Kit wanted to make a [4] s_____________ (yvrsoa) dish, but he used sugar instead of salt. Then he made a very strange [5] m_____________ (xim) of milk and pasta. I didn't [6] d_____________ (read) try it because it looked so bad. In the end, he decided his dish wasn't [7] e_____________ (lbidee) and he had to start over.

B Read and circle the correct option.

I love durians! They're big fruits covered in [1] **spikes** / **tricks** / **tips**! They really [2] **copy** / **stink** / **bend**, so some countries [3] **dare** / **move** / **ban** them from public transportation. They aren't very [4] **up-to-date** / **well known** / **give up** in my country because they don't grow here. I'd like to have a [5] **spike** / **review** / **greenhouse** so I could try to grow a durian seed. But my sister said that I would [6] **give up** / **join in** / **dare** because durians are hard to grow!

C Complete the dialogues with a short answer.

1 **A:** Do you enjoy swimming in the ocean?
  B: Yes, I _____________ .

2 **A:** Could Charlie ride a horse when he was five?
  B: No, he _____________ .

3 **A:** Are we going out soon?
  B: Yes, we _____________ .

4 **A:** Has your teacher ever been to Peru?
  B: Yes, she _____________ .

5 **A:** Will you study French next semester?
  B: No, I _____________ .

Think and Reflect: Unit 10

My understanding of knowledge ☆☆☆☆☆

How well I achieved my goal for Unit 10 ☆☆☆☆☆

The most interesting thing that I learned _________________________________

My goal for Unit 11 _________________________________

11 How can our prior knowledge help us?

Vocabulary 1

A Complete the sentences.

hoard   curator   reward   exhibition   cabinet   emperor

1 Please put the cups in the kitchen __________.

2 This is a beautiful statue of a Roman __________.

3 If you find the gold ring that she lost, she'll give you a __________.

4 There is an interesting __________ at the museum this week.

5 Look at this incredible __________ of treasure!

6 The __________ is showing us around the museum.

B Match to make sentences.

1 If you stumble, …

2 If you find a priceless watch, …

3 If you squeeze the water bottle, …

4 If you scrape your knee, …

5 If you are staring in disbelief, …

6 If you eat a dozen eggs, …

a you should report it to the police.

b you might get a stomachache.

c you will need to clean it.

d you might fall.

e you might be at the Taj Mahal in Agra.

f you might get wet.

A **Complete the sentences with the correct form of *look* or *look like*.**

1 You ___________________________ tired. Did you stay up late?

2 One girl in my class ___________________________ my sister.

3 What does the moon ___________________________ up close?

4 Everyone says she ___________________________ cool in these sneakers.

5 He ___________________________ his twin brother.

6 Do chimpanzees and orangutans ___________________________ exactly the same?

B **Read and write *Active* or *Passive*.**

1 Many people **visit** my country every year.   ___________________

2 They **are shown** around the capital, Lisbon.   ___________________

3 They **are told** about the history and culture of the city.   ___________________

4 Often they **take** trips to other cities, such as Óbidos and Porto.   ___________________

5 They **see** ancient castles and interesting museums.   ___________________

6 They enjoy going to restaurants where our traditional music **is played**.   ___________________

C **Complete the active and passive sentences.**

> display   is grown   discover   is spoken   make   grow   are celebrated
> are discovered   is made   speak   are displayed   celebrate

1 People _______________ pasta all over the world.

   Pasta _______________ all over the world.

2 Old objects _______________ in museums.

   Museums _______________ old objects.

3 New plants and animals _______________ every year.

   People _______________ new plants and animals every year.

4 People _______________ corn in many countries.

   Corn _______________ in many countries.

5 Many festivals _______________ in my country.

   People _______________ many festivals in my country.

6 People _______________ Spanish in Mexico and Spain.

   Spanish _______________ in Mexico and Spain.

What can tourists enjoy seeing or doing in your country?

When I visited New York last year, I discovered that it
1 _______________ (call) *The Big Apple*. The city **2** _______________ (visit)
by millions of tourists every year! Like many cities around the
world, New York **3** _______________ (know) for its famous buildings.
Sometimes there are long lines to see them! Tickets for many of
the main attractions **4** _______________ (sell) online, but you can
also buy them on the day of your visit. Several times a day, tourists
5 _______________ (take) by boat to see the famous Statue of Liberty.
I like New York at night when all the lights **6** _______________ (switch)
on. It looks fantastic.

E **Unscramble the sentences.**

1 nature reserve / many / saw / We / animals / in the

   ____

2 three times / The / fed / a day / animals / are

   ____

3 are / health checks / They / given / by a vet / regular

   ____

4 shown / Visitors / are / nature reserve / the / around

   ____

5 pictures and videos / A lot of / taken / are

   ____

6 rest and play / can / The / animals / in the / nature reserve

   ____

F **Complete the sentences in the chart.**

	Active	Passive
1	Do people often find treasure?	Is treasure often _______________ ?
2	Where do people _______________ ?	Where is treasure found?
3	People teach history in school.	_______________ in school.
4	People _______________ .	Documentaries are made about wildlife.
5	Farmers grow apple trees on farms.	_______________ on farms.
6	People build houses in cities.	_______________ in cities.

A 🔧 **Look at the pictures and title of the adventure story. What do you want to know? Write four questions.**

1 ____
2 ____
3 ____
4 ____

B **Read the adventure story. What did the children lead the archeologists to find?**

The Queen of Chiapas

Every year, Alina and her brother, Leon, looked forward to adventure camp. It was always a week filled with surprises and fun. This year, adventure camp was in the Lacandón rainforest in Chiapas, Mexico, a place well known for its plants, waterfalls, and ancient ruins.

On the first day, Leon, Alina, their friends, and the camp leaders set off to learn about rainforest flowers. They hiked a few kilometers along a path, taking notes and pictures of everything they saw.

"Let's take a break. It's very hot and wet in the rainforest," said Alina, sitting down on a rock. "What's this?" she asked, pulling Leon toward her.

"It looks like … Oh! It looks like a drawing, or maybe writing?" replied Leon, scraping the dirt to see more easily. "And there are more drawings over there!"

Leon walked a few meters and stumbled. "Ouch!" he said. "There's a massive rock here!"

The two children began to explore. After a few minutes, it was clear that there was not just one rock, but two huge rocks forming a gate or entrance.

Alina's eyes opened wide in disbelief. *An entrance to what?* she wondered.

"Look at these hieroglyphs. This has to be a Mayan ruin," said Leon. "I think we've discovered something that's hundreds of years old."

At that moment, sunlight shone through the tall trees.

"Look, now I can see that the bottom of the entrance is blocked by big rocks," Alina gasped.

"Yes, and it's also blocked by roots and vines," replied Leon. "There's no way we can go any further. Let's go and find the camp leaders."

The brother and sister ran back to the group. "Come quickly!" They shouted. "We've found a ruin!"

A week later, archeologists from several countries arrived in the rainforest. After months of carefully clearing rocks and vines, they finally got a reward for their hard work. Behind the entrance was a staircase, leading to several underground tunnels and rooms.

The team of archeologists checked every centimeter of every room. They found several hoards of jewelry. There were priceless necklaces, earrings, and rings. Then, at the end of the longest tunnel, they found a room with a tomb! It was the lost tomb of Lady Six Sky, a powerful queen from the seventh century.

"I can't wait for next year's adventure camp," said Alina.

Leon smiled. "I wonder what we might discover next!"

C **Underline these words in the text.**

> priceless   stumbled   disbelief   reward   scraping   hoards

D **Look at your questions from A. Write the answers you found.**

1 ____

2 ____

3 ____

4 ____

E **Answer the questions.**

1 Where does the story take place?

____

2 What is the weather like?

____

3 What three things are blocking the entrance?

____

4 Who finds the staircase?

____

5 What priceless things do they find in the underground rooms?

____

6 Whose tomb do the archeologists find?

____

Have you ever found something unusual? What was it?

A Check (✓) the correct option.

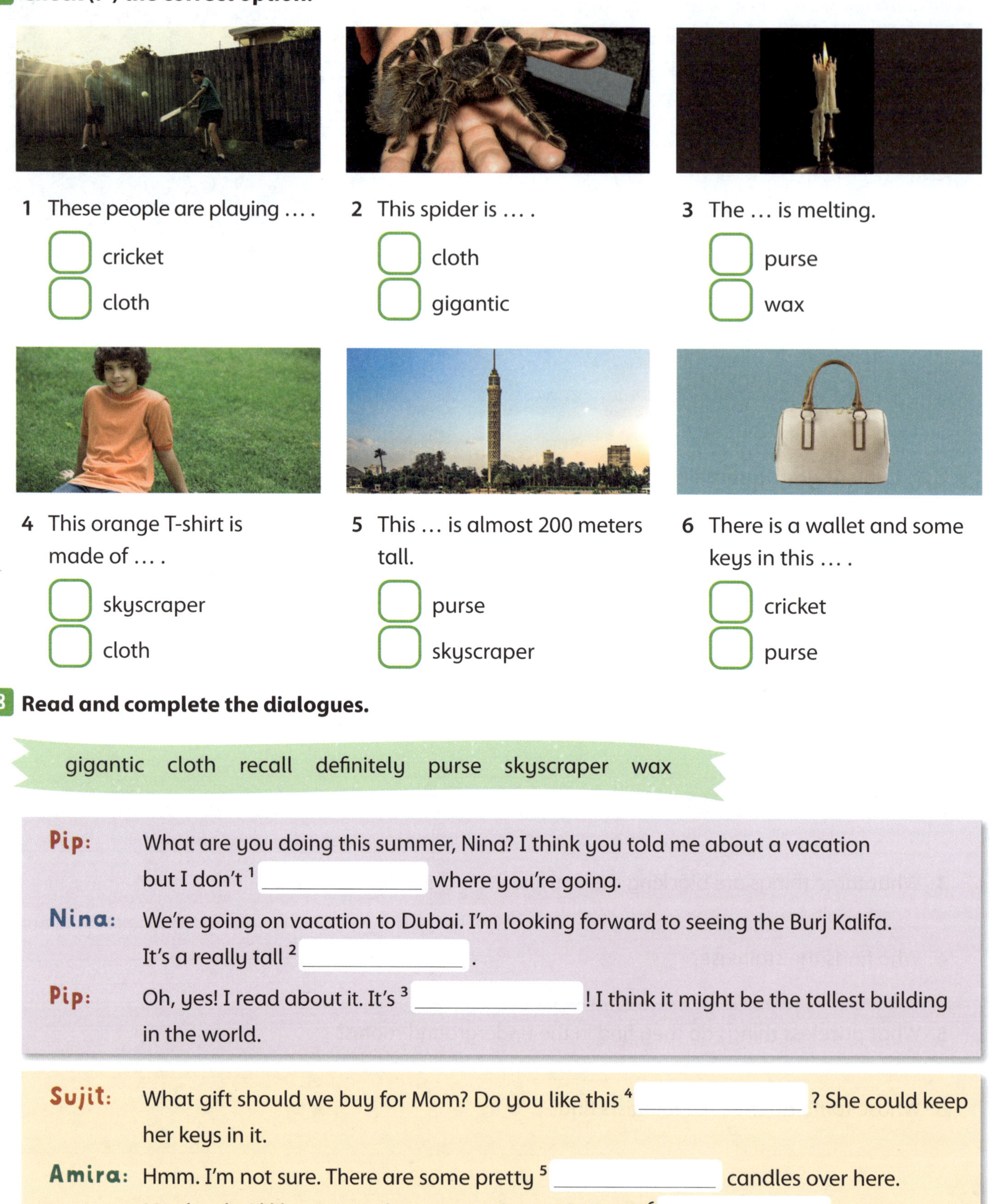

1 These people are playing … .
- ☐ cricket
- ☐ cloth

2 This spider is … .
- ☐ cloth
- ☐ gigantic

3 The … is melting.
- ☐ purse
- ☐ wax

4 This orange T-shirt is made of … .
- ☐ skyscraper
- ☐ cloth

5 This … is almost 200 meters tall.
- ☐ purse
- ☐ skyscraper

6 There is a wallet and some keys in this … .
- ☐ cricket
- ☐ purse

B Read and complete the dialogues.

gigantic   cloth   recall   definitely   purse   skyscraper   wax

Pip: What are you doing this summer, Nina? I think you told me about a vacation but I don't ¹ _______________ where you're going.

Nina: We're going on vacation to Dubai. I'm looking forward to seeing the Burj Kalifa. It's a really tall ² _______________ .

Pip: Oh, yes! I read about it. It's ³ _______________ ! I think it might be the tallest building in the world.

Sujit: What gift should we buy for Mom? Do you like this ⁴ _______________ ? She could keep her keys in it.

Amira: Hmm. I'm not sure. There are some pretty ⁵ _______________ candles over here. Maybe she'd like one. Or there's some beautiful batik ⁶ _______________ .

Sujit: Yes, that's stunning. Mom would ⁷ _______________ love to make something from that.

Vocabulary 3

A **Read and circle the correct option.**

It's my first day at summer camp. I feel a little [1] **homesick / zip-lining** and I [2] **understandable / miss** my family. Mom said it was [3] **homesick / understandable** to feel [4] **anxious / miss** at first. I think I'll be OK because I really enjoy going for [5] **zip-lining / sleepovers** at my friends' houses. There are many fun things to do at camp, including treasure hunts, cooking on a camp fire, and even [6] **anxious / zip-lining**!

B **Complete the sentences.**

zip-lining   sleepover   homesick   anxious   understandable   miss

1 Do you feel ________________ when you take a test?

2 We love going for a ________________ with friends!

3 It's ________________ that the neighbor is upset about his flowers.

4 I sometimes get ________________ when I'm not with my family.

5 I won't see my grandparents again for months. I'm going to ________________ them.

6 I love adventurous activities, but ________________ is my favorite!

A Correct the sentences. Use commas and colons.

1   I like fruit, apples: bananas and oranges.

2   We play many different sports baseball: soccer, and tennis.

3   This cake: has a lot of ingredients butter, sugar, flour and raisins.

4   I have several classes I enjoy in school science English and math.

B Read the sentences. Rewrite them as one sentence, using colons.

1   I'm taking several objects to school today. I'm taking a ruler, a backpack, and tennis shoes.

I'm taking several objects to school today: a ruler, a backpack, and tennis shoes.

2   We need some ingredients for the salad. We need lettuce, tomatoes, cucumber, and carrots.

3   I need many things for summer camp. I need a flashlight, a sleeping bag, and snacks.

4   Many crops are grown in my country. Rice, beans, and corn are all grown here.

5   We saw many birds in the nature reserve. We saw parrots, toucans, crows, and hawks.

C Write a paragraph about a place you've learned about and what you want to learn more about. Use colons to show lists.

This week, we learned about Australia. It's a gigantic island with many things to see: coral reefs, waterfalls, mountains, and beaches. There are famous cities, too: Melbourne, Sydney, and Canberra. I want to learn more about the wildlife in Australia: kangaroos, crocodiles, wombats, and koalas! Koalas look really cute. I'd love to see one in the wild.

A **Unscramble the words to complete the paragraph.**

I was playing ¹ c_____________ (ickcret) with a friend when I found an old coin in my yard.
When I saw the coin in the dirt, I just stared at it in ² d_____________ (iefbdlise). Next,
I ³ s_____________ (deprasc) the dirt off it and cleaned it with some ⁴ c_____________ (toclh).
It looked shiny! It's ⁵ d_____________ (niftydeeli) very old because it doesn't look like any of the
coins I've seen before. I plan to take the coin to the ⁶ c_____________ (rotracu) at our local museum.

B **Read and complete the paragraph.**

> sleepover   understandable   cabinet   miss   homesick   recall

Do you ever feel ¹ _____________ when you go to a new place? I do! I think it's ² _____________
to feel this way because you ³ _____________ your family and friends. I ⁴ _____________ going
for a ⁵ _____________ at my friend's house when I was little. I saw a big spider in the kitchen
⁶ _____________ and I got scared!

C **Rewrite the active sentences as passive sentences.**

1   Scientists study many different plants around the world.

   <u>Many different plants around the world are studied.</u>

2   They often discover a new species.

   ____

3   They write a report about the plants.

   ____

4   Governments protect plants and trees in national parks.

   ____

5   Guides show visitors around the national parks.

   ____

Think and Reflect: Unit 11

My understanding of knowledge ☆☆☆☆☆

How well I achieved my goal for Unit 11 ☆☆☆☆☆

The most interesting thing that I learned ____

My goal for Unit 12 ____

Vocabulary 1

A **Complete the sentences.**

> fragment   project   compost   type   toxic   guidance

1 If you _______________ too fast, you'll spell words wrong.

2 I've been trying to repair the broken cup, but I've lost one _______________ .

3 This building's always nice, but it's prettier when they _______________ colorful designs on to it!

4 People who work there have to wear safety equipment because of the _______________ gases.

5 It was a difficult assignment, but her _______________ really helped me.

6 We _______________ our food waste and use it in the garden later.

B **Write something to replace the underlined words, so that the sentences are true for you.**

1 I often have a feeling of frustration when <u>I make mistakes on the piano</u>. _______________

2 I sometimes whisper when <u>I'm in a movie theater</u>. _______________

3 There's a lot of junk in <u>the cabinet in my living room</u>. _______________

4 I'll be very happy if someone delivers <u>a pizza to my house tonight</u>. _______________

5 My favorite spherical objects are <u>oranges</u>. _______________

6 I urgently have to <u>eat something – I'm really hungry</u>. _______________

Word Study and Grammar

A **Complete the compound adjectives.**

> dollar   page   minute   course   hour   story   word   day

1 We had a delicious three-_______________ meal: cheese salad, then chicken, then ice cream. 😊

2 It's a four-_______________ train journey from here to the capital. 🚂

3 My aunt lives right at the top of an eight-_______________ building, and her view of the city is fantastic! 😍

4 My mom works a five-_______________ week. She never has to work on Fridays or Saturdays. 😄

5 My grandma wrote me a two-_______________ letter all about her childhood on a farm. 🦌

6 I have to write a fifty-_______________ story for homework, and I'm going to give it a mountain setting. 🏔️

7 I lost my purse, but luckily it only had a one-_______________ bill and a pen in it. 😌

8 There was a 15-_______________ break in the middle of the soccer game. ⚽

B **Read and circle the correct option.**

1 All the cakes that were **baked** / **bake** / **baking** for the party were **eat** / **ate** / **eaten** , but the orange juice wasn't **drunk** / **drank** / **drink** .

2 The photo was **took** / **taken** / **take** on my mom's phone, but then it was **forgotten** / **forget** / **forgot** . It wasn't **print** / **printing** / **printed** .

3 I was **given** / **gave** / **give** some beautiful gloves for my eighth birthday. They were **make** / **made** / **making** of wool and they were very warm. But unfortunately they were **leaving** / **left** / **leave** on the bus by my brother last year and they were never **see** / **saw** / **seen** again.

C **Unscramble the questions and write the answers.**

1 yesterday / it / done / Was ✓
Was it done yesterday?
Yes, it was.

2 the / delivered / Were / books ✗
____

3 were / How / languages / spoken / many 4
____

4 she / in / Was / the / hurt / accident ✗
____

5 the / broken / Were / all / glasses ✓
____

6 homework / was / your / When / finished 🕐
____

1 Li Bai wrote this poem.

→ This poem ___was written by Li Bai___ .

2 Pelé scored all the goals.

→ All the goals ___________________________ .

3 Senna drove that car.

→ That car ___________________________ .

4 Shakira didn't sing that song.

→ That song ___________________________ .

5 Kipchoge ran the fastest marathon.

→ The fastest marathon

___________________________ .

6 Al-Jazari didn't design those clocks.

→ Those clocks ___________________________ .

E **Complete the sentences in the chart.**

	Active	Passive
1	Manon ___________________ a picture.	A picture was drawn by Manon.
2	My parents didn't send the email.	The email ___________________ my parents.
3	They ___________________ the trees.	The trees weren't planted.
4	Stan changed the plans.	The plans ___________________ Stan.
5	___________ anyone ___________ it?	Was it chosen?
6	Did people know the facts?	___________ the facts ___________ ?

F **Write about things that were done by you and people you know. Use the past passive of the verbs in parentheses.**

1 The cake was baked by my sister. ___________________ (bake)

2 ____ (eat)

3 ____ (drink)

4 ____ (repair)

5 ____ (give)

A **Read the science-fiction story. How did Delma and Sovani help each other?**

Delma and the Purple Weed

Delma was worried. Planet Zob used to be covered in zobelias. These delicate red plants kept the planet healthy, and they were also delicious to eat! Now a toxic purple weed was spreading all over the planet, and the zobelias were dying fast. The people of Zob urgently needed a solution to the problem, but nothing seemed to work.

"Let's ask Planet Narbo for guidance!" Delma said one evening in frustration.

"No way!" replied her father. "The weed was probably sent to Zob by the Narbians in the first place." Planet Narbo was the nearest planet to Planet Zob, but the Zobians hated the Narbians. The two planets became enemies so long ago that no one could even remember why.

But Delma had to try to save her planet. That night, she projected her image on to a wall in a street on Narbo, using her spherical communication device. "Hi," she said nervously, waving at a boy and his mom. "Do you have time to talk?"

They smiled and nodded. The boy was called Sovani. He seemed friendly – nothing like the Narbians that everyone on Zob talked about. "You look cold," Delma said. "Is it winter on Narbo?"

"It's always winter here, and we're always cold!" Sovani replied. "We used to make the fabric for our clothes from strundel trees, but all our strundel trees were cut down by the people in charge of our planet. We don't know how to make warm fabric now! Every day, I take care of our vegetable garden in the freezing cold, wearing just a thin shirt. I'd love to feel warm again!"

"I'll ask other Zobians for ideas," said Delma, kindly. "By the way, do you have weeds in your vegetable garden? A purple weed is growing all over Zob!"

"Of course. But we put special weedkiller on our weeds. You're welcome to the recipe," smiled Sovani.

B Underline these words in the text.

spherical   projected   toxic   frustration   urgently   guidance

C Number the events in the correct order.

a ☐ Delma gave Sovani some useful information from Zob.

b ☐ Purple weeds started to kill important plants on Zob.

c ☐ Sovani gave Delma some useful information from Narbo.

d ☐ Delma was told that the Narbians might be responsible for the purple weeds.

e ☐ Delma discovered that people on Narbo were cold.

f ☐ Delma used her communication device to communicate for the first time with Narbians.

g ☐ Zob and Narbo became enemies.

D Answer the questions.

1 What do you think the author's purpose is? Check (✓) the correct box(es).

☐ to persuade   ☐ to inform   ☐ to entertain

2 Why did you check the box(es) that you did?

____

3 What similarities are there between the problems on the planets in the story and the problems on Earth? Do you think the author created the similarities on purpose? Why? / Why not?

____

4 How do you think the author feels about sharing knowledge?

____

Do you enjoy reading sci-fi stories? Why? / Why not?

A **Match to make sentences.**

1 He's studying botany because he loves …   **a** a yacht.
2 They went on a voyage on …   **b** plants.
3 I'd love to run …   **c** footprint.
4 A lot of frogs live …   **d** in these wetlands.
5 I want to reduce my environmental …   **e** the 1980s.
6 This school was founded in …   **f** a business one day.

B **Read and complete the blog post.**

found   sustainably   run   specialized   wetlands   botany

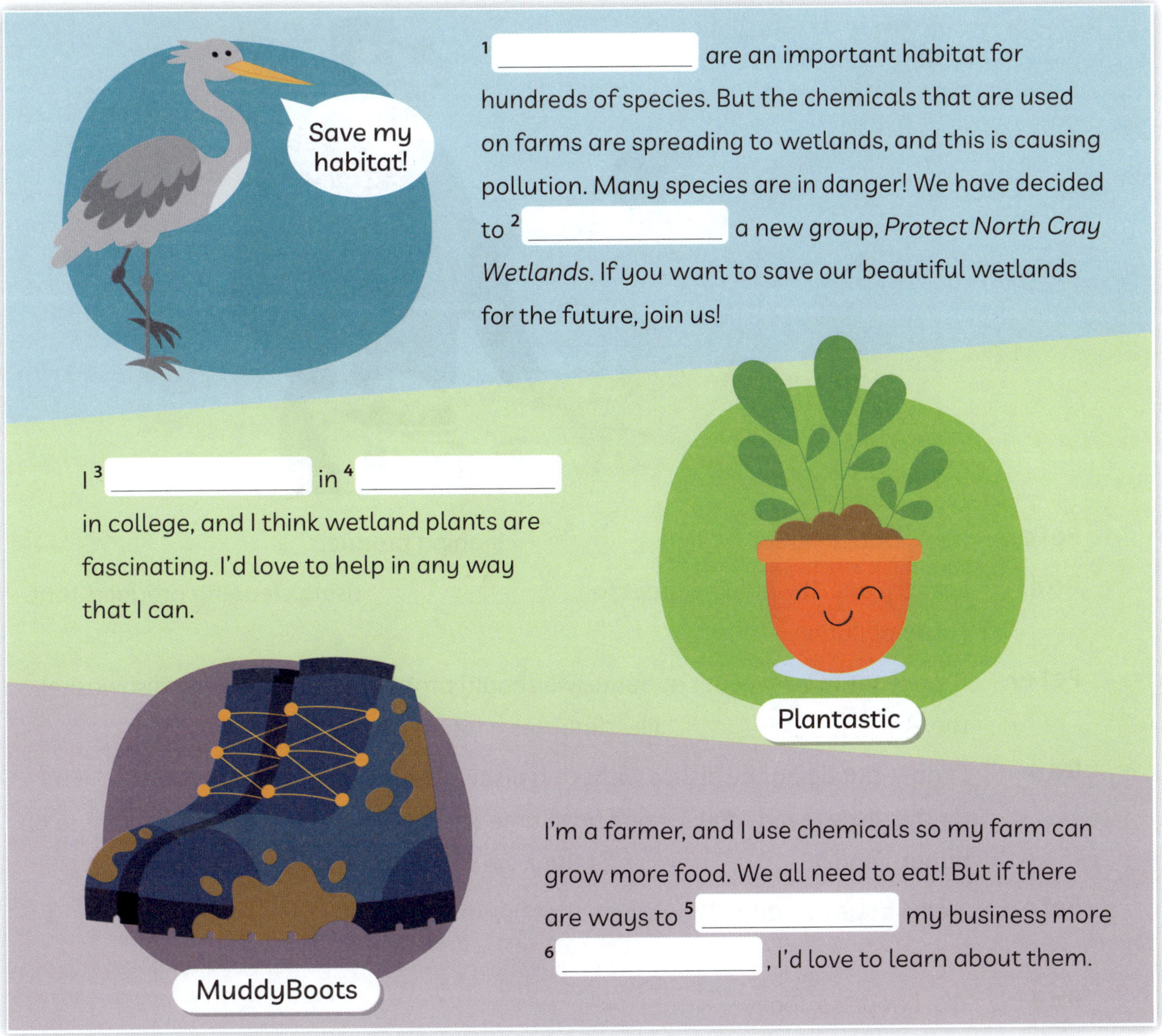

1 ________________ are an important habitat for hundreds of species. But the chemicals that are used on farms are spreading to wetlands, and this is causing pollution. Many species are in danger! We have decided to 2 ________________ a new group, *Protect North Cray Wetlands*. If you want to save our beautiful wetlands for the future, join us!

I 3 ________________ in 4 ________________ in college, and I think wetland plants are fascinating. I'd love to help in any way that I can.

I'm a farmer, and I use chemicals so my farm can grow more food. We all need to eat! But if there are ways to 5 ________________ my business more 6 ________________ , I'd love to learn about them.

A **Read and circle *True* or *False*.**

1 Biodegradable things take thousands of years to decompose. True   False
2 Under-nourished people have enough food to eat. True   False
3 TVs and refrigerators are examples of appliances. True   False
4 If you avoid doing something, you do it badly. True   False
5 Your labor is the work that you do. True   False
6 If something is available at a store, people can buy it there. True   False

B **Read and complete the dialogue.**

available   biodegradable   avoid   labor   under-nourished   appliance

Peter: Look, Dad, they sell [1] ________________ cleaning products.

Dad: Let's try one. It would be great to [2] ________________ using cleaning products that cause pollution.

Peter: If we want to be greener at home, we should probably stop using our dishwasher, too. An [3] ________________ like that uses a lot of electricity.

Dad: I know, but doing the dishes without a dishwasher is hard [4] ________________ ! If I do the dishes every day, I won't have time to cook dinner. So unless you want to be hungry and [5] ________________ , I think we should keep using the dishwasher.

Peter: Well, I hope one day dishwashers that use much less electricity will be [6] ________________ .

Dad: Yes, I hope so, too.

A **Read the persuasive email. Label the different sections.**

Explanation   Introduction   Consequences of no action   Closing
Request for action   Subject line   Opening   Topic sentence

______________ **Subject: Let's Make Fashion Sustainable!**

______________ Dear Fashion Business Leader,

______________ I am writing to you because I have found out that the fashion business is responsible for a lot of environmental damage.

____
______________ The fashion business damages the environment in several ways. The way that fabric is produced wastes a lot of water, and fabric dyes can cause water pollution. Clothes are often made on the other side of the world from where they are bought, so there is air and water pollution from transportation, too. Also, clothes are sometimes only worn for a short time before they are thrown away. But the fabrics aren't biodegradable.

______________ Unless action is taken, the world's environmental problems will continue to get worse. One day we will find that there is no safe water to drink, no clean air to breathe, and nowhere to go that isn't covered in trash.

______________ I am asking you to take action to reduce the environmental damage from fashion. You could support the use of biodegradable fabrics that are produced sustainably. And you could support the buying and selling of second-hand clothes, so people change their fashion choices without an environmental cost. Please help to make fashion sustainable!

______________ Sincerely,
Oscar Sanz

B **Complete the sentences.**

1 To open his email, Oscar starts with the word ______________ .

2 In his introduction paragraph, Oscar says why he ______________ .

3 In the next paragraph, Oscar gives reasons why the fashion business ______________ .

4 In the last paragraph, Oscar suggests ways that people in the fashion business can ______________ .

5 To close his email, Oscar uses the word ______________ and his name.

C You're going to write a persuasive email about another environmental problem. Brainstorm. Write your ideas in the chart below.

Environmental problems	Possible solutions

D Choose an environmental problem. Do some research and plan your email by completing the chart.

Subject line:

Email to:

Explanation of the problem:

Consequences of no action:

Action(s) that you request:

E Now write the first draft of your persuasive email in your notebook. 

- Include a subject line that grabs your reader's attention.
- Start your email with an opening.
- State clearly why you are writing.
- Explain the current situation.
- Use topic sentences to state the main idea of each paragraph.
- Make your reader feel strongly about the consequences of no action.
- Explain what you want your reader to do.
- End your email with a closing.

F Check your work and make any necessary changes.

- Did you do everything in the list in **E**?
- Is your grammar, spelling, and punctuation correct?
- Is your writing clear and easy for other people to understand?

G Now write the final draft of your persuasive email in your notebook. 

A Read and circle the correct option.

Emilia started to [1] **type** / **run** / **found** instructions on the computer: "How to [2] **project** / **labor** / **compost** your food waste." She was writing the instructions for her class's website about living more [3] **sustainably** / **toxic** / **urgently**. Her friends were preparing [4] **frustration** / **wetlands** / **guidance** on other environmentally-friendly options. For example, Dani was writing about bags made of [5] **under-nourished** / **spherical** / **biodegradable** materials instead of plastic, and Shen was writing about repairing and recycling electrical [6] **appliances** / **whispers** / **botany**.

B Unscramble the words to complete the paragraph.

Can you see those pieces of wood on the beach? They're the [1] f_____________ (tsgmerfan) of an old ship. Long ago, a lot of Chinese craftspeople [2] s_____________ (pealdecsiiz) in making beautiful blue and white pots. Those pots were [3] a_____________ (ilvalabae) in markets around the world. The ship was on a [4] v_____________ (avygeo) to [5] d_____________ (vderlie) some of the pots to Europe, but there was a storm. The ship was blown toward some rocks near this beach, and it couldn't [6] a_____________ (dioav) them. It was completely destroyed.

C Find and cross out a mistake in each past passive sentence. Write the correct word.

1 The Great Wall of China didn't built by the Romans. _______________

2 This webpage was wrote by my friend. _______________

3 The cookies be baked yesterday. _______________

4 How was you hurt? _______________

5 The children were driving here by their mom. _______________

Think and Reflect: Unit 12

My understanding of knowledge ☆☆☆☆☆

How well I achieved my goal for Unit 12 ☆☆☆☆☆

The most interesting thing that I learned _______________________________________

My goal for Unit 13 _______________________________________

Vocabulary 1

A **Complete the sentences.**

germinate   slippery   sunburn   extract   absorb   dehydration

1 The sponge will _______________ the water I knocked over.

2 Watch out! The sidewalk is wet so it's very _______________.

3 You might get _______________ if you stay outside too long today.

4 The seeds I planted have started to _______________.

5 Be sure to drink plenty of water to avoid _______________.

6 Most plants _______________ nutrients from the soil.

B **Match the definitions to the words or phrases.**

1 You will be horizontal when you do this.   •

2 You have a host when you do this.   •

3 You sometimes need to overcome this.   •

4 You've probably gotten this characteristic from your parents.   •

5 You will use a large quantity of this if you take a bath.   •

6 You access a room by opening this.   •

• **a** stay over at your friend's house

• **b** a problem or challenge in your life

• **c** water

• **d** lie down in bed

• **e** a door

• **f** the color of your eyes

A **Circle the correct option.**

1 The bus is **stationary** / **stationery**. It isn't moving.

2 What **affect** / **effect** does the sun have on our skin?

3 Let's put the tablet in this bag so we don't **loose** / **lose** it.

4 Valli doesn't like sweet things so she won't have any **dessert** / **desert**.

5 All my friends live near my home, **accept** / **except** for one.

6 I need your **advice** / **advise**. Should I send Pietro a card or an email?

7 We went to the movies and our parents came, **too** / **to**.

8 We need some more **flower** / **flour** to make these cookies.

B **Check (✓) the correct option.**

1 He feels … about the issue.

☐ strong   ☐ strongly

2 Our teachers are always … .

☐ patiently   ☐ patient

3 I … enjoy hot weather.

☐ usual   ☐ usually

4 My friend is very … .

☐ kindly   ☐ kind

5 The flowers are … .

☐ beautiful   ☐ beautifully

6 I didn't study, so I did … on the test.

☐ bad   ☐ badly

C **Read and complete the story.**

always   nervously   politely   loudly   quickly   angrily   kindly   never

Satomi was late. She packed her backpack **1** ________________ and ran out of the front door, closing it **2** ________________ behind her. Her brother hated noise.

"Don't do that!" he shouted **3** ________________ . But Satomi didn't hear him. Satomi was **4** ________________ late for school. She **5** ________________ set an alarm so that she woke up at the correct time. Unfortunately, her alarm didn't go off today. She got on the bus and saw an empty seat next to Mrs. Mai, her neighbor.

"May I sit here?" she asked **6** ________________ .

"Of course," replied Mrs. Mai, smiling **7** ________________ at Satomi. "But why aren't you going to school today?" Satomi looked at Mrs. Mai.

"I AM going to school! Isn't this the school bus?" she asked, **8** ________________ . Mrs. Mai shook her head.

"No. This is the bus to the airport."

D **Unscramble the sentences.**

1 my / I / slowly / like / lunch / to eat

____

2 hungry / sometimes / feel / I

____

3 always / some / I / vegetables / eat / fresh

____

4 enjoy / eating / I / healthily

____

5 don't / I / eat / junk food / often

____

6 well / My sister / cooks

____

E **Rewrite the sentences with the adverb and the correct form of the in parentheses.**

1 Our teacher (never / be) late for class.

____

2 I (often / meet) my friends on the weekend.

____

3 My brother (sometimes / help) me with my homework.

____

4 I (usually / be) excited to be in coding club.

____

5 The school bus (always / arrive) at 8:10 a.m.

____

F **Write sentences that are true for you. Use an adjective or adverb, as described in parentheses.**

1 (adjective) _______________________________________

2 (adverb of manner) _______________________________________

3 (adverb of frequency) _______________________________________

What Do Plants Know About the World?

Unlike people, plants don't have eyes, ears, or noses. Does that mean they can't experience the world around them? No, not at all! Some plants have very impressive sensing abilities. Read on to discover the incredible characteristics of these fascinating plants.

The sun-loving sunflower

Sunflowers are famous for their ability to sense and follow the movement of the sun. We call this ability *heliotropism*.

In the morning, when the sun rises, young sunflowers face east to capture and absorb the sunlight. During the day, the sunflowers slowly turn and follow the sun's path across the sky. By facing the sun all day, the sunflower accesses plenty of sunlight. At night, the young sunflowers return to face east, ready for the next morning's sunrise. As the sunflowers grow older and stronger, they stop following the sun and stay facing east.

Young sunflowers need a huge amount of sunlight to grow and produce energy, and that's a big challenge for them. Heliotropism helps them to overcome this challenge.

Did you know?

Sunflowers can extract toxic material from the soil to keep the environment clean.

The touch me not plant

This fascinating plant reacts to touch. When you touch the leaves of a *Mimosa pudica* plant, the small leaves (called leaflets) of the plant fold in, like the pages of a book shutting. Then the whole leaf hangs down. After the leaves fold, they usually recover quickly and return to their open position. Scientists think that this adaptation helps the plants defend themselves against herbivores. When an animal tries to eat the leaves, the sudden folding and hanging surprises the herbivore and encourages it to go away.

The eat me not plant

This plant reacts to the sound and feeling of caterpillars chewing its leaves! Scientists have discovered that the *Arabidopsis thaliana* plant can sense the difference between sound vibrations caused by wind and those caused by a hungry caterpillar. In an experiment, they played recordings of the sound of wind and the sound of caterpillars eating. When the wind recording was played, the *Arabidopsis thaliana* didn't react. But when the sound of a caterpillar eating was played, the plant sent out large quantities of a special chemical – mustard oil – which the insects don't like.

B **Underline these words in the text.**

accesses   characteristics   extract   overcome   quantities   absorb

C **Circle the correct answer.**

1 What does heliotropism mean?

  a producing energy   **b** extracting toxic material   **c** following the sun

2 What can sunflowers extract from the soil?

  a sunlight   **b** energy   **c** toxic material

3 What does *Mimosa pudica* react to?

  a touch   **b** heat   **c** noise

4 What threat does *Mimosa pudica* need to overcome?

  a lack of nutrients   **b** being eaten by herbivores   **c** too much sun

5 What happens when *Arabidopsis thaliana* senses a caterpillar eating it?

  a it sends out a chemical   **b** it folds up and hangs   **c** it chews the insects

6 What happens when *Arabidopsis thaliana* hears the sound of wind?

  a it folds up and hangs   **b** it doesn't react   **c** it stops growing

D **Think about the science text. Circle the correct option.**

1 The first paragraph presents **one of the examples** / **the main idea**.

2 The text includes **examples of the main idea** / **causes and effects**.

3 The writer wrote the text to **describe a concept** / **explain a problem**.

Which plant adaptations do you find the most interesting? Why?

A **Match to make sentences.**

1 Ducks and swans have webbed …
2 There are paw …
3 Good tires on a car grip …
4 The baker wears heat-resistant …
5 She is an extraordinary …
6 There's a big hump …

a on the camel's back.
b prints on the ground.
c gloves to protect his hands.
d feet.
e pianist and has a beautiful voice.
f the road well.

B **Read and complete the blog post.**

conditions extraordinary grip pitch

I really like this little bird, the house wren. I like to watch it [1] _______________ the branch of a tree with its feet and start to sing. Scientists like me are researching some of the [2] _______________ birds that have begun to sing at a higher [3] _______________ than usual. Did you know that they do this because they live in noisy [4] _______________ ? All around them, there's the noise of traffic, airplanes, and construction work. This means that they need to sing a lot louder and longer to hear each other!

A **Check (✓) the correct option.**

1 The … in the mountains can affect people's health.

☐ average   ☐ altitude

2 The … temperature here is 16 degrees Celsius, but it can be a lot colder in the winter.

☐ altitude   ☐ average

3 I always … when it's very cold.

☐ raise   ☐ shiver

4 Our teacher showed us how to work … on our own.

☐ efficiently   ☐ average

5 I study hard because I want to … good grades.

☐ maintain   ☐ raise

6 Please … your hand if you know the answer to this question.

☐ maintain   ☐ raise

B **Read and circle *True* or *False*. Correct the false sentences.**

1 You can raise a flag on a flagpole.   True   False

____

2 In a group of friends, the average height is somewhere between the tallest and the shortest.   True   False

____

3 People who work efficiently waste a lot of time.   True   False

____

4 You shiver to cool your body down.   True   False

____

5 To maintain your energy, you need to eat.   True   False

____

6 When you're next to the ocean, you're at a high altitude.   True   False

____

A Unscramble the words to complete the sentences.

1 I live in Egypt. Right now, it's summer and it's u_______________ (ibleebynvlau) hot!

2 You are a_______________ (bysoeluatl) right! Tigers don't live in Africa.

3 My sister plays the drums e_______________ (xetrymele) well.

4 I'm not great at math, but I'm v_______________ (eryv) good at science.

5 Dad didn't sleep well so he's r_______________ (erlyal) tired.

B Check (✓) the sentences that use the adverbs of degree correctly.

1 ◻ I'm extremely happy to see you!

2 ◻ It's absolutely cold this morning.

3 ◻ We did really well in our exams.

4 ◻ You get unbelievably good grades in English.

5 ◻ This is an absolutely good movie.

6 ◻ Our teacher is very kind.

C Write a paragraph about a place you've visited. Use the adverbs of degree *very*, *really*, *absolutely*, *extremely*, and *unbelievably*.

Last summer, I went to a new park near my grandparents' house. I was really excited to go because it has many extremely old trees. My grandpa said that one of the trees was more than 400 years old! We went to find it. It's absolutely huge, with a thick trunk and very long branches. I'd like to know exactly when it was planted, who planted it, and why. It's an unbelievably beautiful tree and I really hope it survives another 400 years.

____

____

____

____

____

A **Read and write *a*, *b*, or *c*.**

1 Penguins don't have ______ but they do have ______ feet.

   a webbed   **b** heat-resistant   **c** paws

2 Plants need to ______ a lot of water to avoid ______.

   a sunburn   **b** dehydration   **c** absorb

3 We stayed with an ______ family when we went to Mexico. They were fantastic ______.

   a extraordinary   **b** slippery   **c** hosts

4 The ______ temperature here is minus 6. It's so cold that it makes everyone ______.

   a average   **b** shiver   **c** horizontal

B **Circle the correct option.**

1 The roots of plants **absorb** / **germinate** water.

2 When it's icy, the sidewalk can be **heat-resistant** / **slippery**.

3 Having brown eyes is a **characteristic** / **condition**.

4 Vertical is the opposite of **webbed** / **horizontal**.

C **Use the adverbs to write sentences that are true for you.**

1 (politely) I speak politely to my friends and family, and when I meet new people.

2 (often) ____

____

3 (angrily) ____

____

4 (carefully) ____

____

5 (always) ____

____

Think and Reflect: Unit 13

My understanding of adaptation ☆☆☆☆☆

How well I achieved my goal for Unit 13 ☆☆☆☆☆

The most interesting thing that I learned ____

My goal for Unit 14 ____

Vocabulary 1

A **Read and complete the paragraphs.**

agriculture   ancestors   remain   breed

I live on a farm. My parents [1]______________ sheep. I love the little lambs that are born every spring. One day I'd like to work in [2]______________ like my parents. I hope I always [3]______________ on the farm of my [4]______________!

preserve   convenience   manufacture

When businesses [5]______________ food products in factories, they often add chemicals that help to [6]______________ the food. Everyone appreciates the [7]______________ of longer-lasting food, but some scientists think that the use of these chemicals is bad for our health.

contaminated   spices   variety   bacteria   digest

My stomach hurts. I ate too much for dinner. We had a curry with meat and a [8]______________ of vegetables and [9]______________ in it. It was delicious, but it will take my body a long time to [10]______________ it! I hope that's the problem, and the food wasn't [11]______________ with dangerous [12]______________!

B **Complete the second sentence so it has a similar meaning to the first.**

variety   manufacture   contaminated   remain   convenience

1 I like eating similar things every day.　　I don't like much ______________ in my food.

2 Tomorrow, it will be hot like today.　　Tomorrow, it will ______________ hot.

3 They make cellphones in that factory.　　They ______________ cellphones in that factory.

4 There are toxic chemicals in the water.　　The water is ______________ with toxic chemicals.

5 I love how easy my walk to school is.　　I love the ______________ of living near my school.

A **Complete the sentences with the correct preposition.**

1 I've never heard ________________ a starfruit before.

2 They thanked him ________________ the delicious meal.

3 We need to think ________________ something nice to cook for lunch.

4 How does Vietnamese food compare ________________ Thai food?

5 We have to wait ________________ Jane before we can eat.

6 I'm looking ________________ a recipe for lemon cookies.

7 I've always dreamed ________________ working in a chocolate factory.

8 My sister thinks bananas taste horrible, and I agree ________________ her.

B **Read and answer *Yes* or *No*.**

1 If I wasn't busy, I would help you cook.

Are you busy? ________________

Are you going to help? ________________

2 They would learn Arabic if they lived in Egypt.

Do they live in Egypt? ________________

Are they learning Arabic? ________________

3 She wouldn't need to walk if she had a bike.

Does she need to walk? ________________

Does she have a bike? ________________

4 If we got lost, we'd ask someone the way.

Are you likely to get lost? ________________

Are you likely to ask someone the way? ________________

C **Circle the correct option.**

1 If he **listens** / **listened** more carefully, he would **learn** / **learned** more.

2 People wouldn't **have** / **had** enough food to eat if there **aren't** / **weren't** any farms.

3 If I **have** / **had** enough money, I'd **eat** / **ate** in this restaurant every day!

4 Would you **become** / **became** a vegetarian if I **ask** / **asked** you to?

5 If Mom **buys** / **bought** us some bread, we would **make** / **made** sandwiches.

6 If they **don't** / **didn't** come to your party, would you **be** / **were** sad?

 Complete the second conditional sentences.

knew   had   moved   grow   be   bake   see   didn't spend

1 If we _______________ a yard, I'd _______________ some vegetables.
2 If he _______________ how to bake, he would _______________ us some bread.
3 I wouldn't _______________ you often if you _______________ to a different city.
4 If we _______________ time with them, would they _______________ lonely?

 Complete the sentences with the correct form of the verbs in parentheses.

1 If you _______________ (be) an orangutan, you _______________ (love) swinging from trees.

2 I _______________ (build) a snowman if it _______________ (snow) today.

3 _______________ (he, come) to my party if I _______________ (invite) him?

4 If we _______________ (not go) to school, we _______________ (get) bored.

5 My little sister _______________ (not clean) her teeth if I _______________ (not tell) her to.

6 If you _______________ (meet) someone famous, what _______________ (you, say) to them?

 Complete the sentences for you.

1 If I could go anywhere in the world, I _____________________________________ .
2 I _____________________________________ if I didn't see my friends very often.
3 I _____________________________________ if I had a lot of money.
4 If I knew how to _______________________ , I _____________________________ .

A **Read the feature article. How is bread different now from when it was first invented?**

Bread: A Journey Through Time

How much bread do you eat? Perhaps you like toast and honey for breakfast, or a sandwich for lunch, or maybe bread with your evening meal? For many of us, eating bread is an important part of our daily routine. But that wasn't always true. Let's take a journey through the history of bread!

Hunter-gatherers

Our early ancestors were hunter-gatherers. They ate the food that they found in their natural environment, including the seeds of wild grasses, called grain. One day, they figured out that they could grind the grain between two stones to make flour. They could then mix the flour with water, and bake a flat type of bread on hot stones! Why bread? Partly for the convenience: bread was easy to carry around in a bag. Cooked grain was also easier for the stomach to digest than raw grain.

On the farm

About 12,000 years ago, agriculture started to become popular. Grains were some of the most common crops, and most farming families made flatbread in their own little bread oven.

Ancient Egypt

The ancient Egyptians discovered something that changed bread for ever: yeast. Yeast is a tiny living thing that eats sugar and produces gas. If it's added to a bread recipe, it can put air into the bread and give it a fluffy texture. Now bread wasn't only flat. It could come in a lot of shapes and sizes.

Did you know?

The ancient Egyptians used moldy bread to treat skin infections. Thousands of years later, 20th-century scientists figured out how to make a medicine from a bread mold called penicillin. It kills bacteria that can make humans ill, and it has saved millions of lives globally.

Indian flatbread

Around the world

In Mexico, the Maya used corn to create breads such as tortillas and tamales. In India, flat breads such as naan and chapatis remained the favorite type. In Europe, there was a lot of variety, including bagels from Poland and long bread sticks from France.

Did you know?

In the Middle Ages, people used stale slices of bread instead of plates!

Factories

In the 20th century, bread making moved from small bakeries to factories. Some bread companies today can manufacture millions of loaves every day! People have been using bread slicing machines since 1928, so these days we don't even need a knife to enjoy a nice slice of bread.

Bread is more than just food; it's a part of our history!

B **Underline these words in the text.**

digest   agriculture   variety   ancestors   manufacture   remained   convenience

C **Read and circle *True* or *False*.**

1 Raw grain was easier to digest than bread.	True	False
2 A lot of the first farmers grew grain.	True	False
3 The texture of bread is different when it has yeast in it.	True	False
4 Penicillin has saved millions of lives in ancient Egypt.	True	False
5 Bread in Mexico was usually made from corn.	True	False
6 In factories, people slice bread with knives.	True	False

D  **Match the main ideas to the details. Then write a summary of the article in your notebook.**

Main ideas

a hunter-gatherers   **b** farming   **c** ancient Egypt   **d** around the world   **e** factories

Details

______ crop
______ wild grass seeds
______ millions of loaves
______ family ovens

______ yeast
______ mold
______ slicing machines
______ flour

______ hot stones
______ corn bread, naan, bagels, and bread sticks

Do you eat a lot of bread? How and when do you like to eat it?

A **Check (✓) the correct option.**

1 The first people of Australia painted beautiful rock art. They often got their paints through … with people from other parts of the country.

☐ wander ☐ trade

2 For …, they liked dancing and playing throwing and catching games.

☐ flatten ☐ entertainment

3 From the 18th century, British people … Australia.

☐ increased ☐ colonized

4 Many British … in Australia were sheep farmers.

☐ settlers ☐ harbors

5 Ships from Sydney's … transported the wool of Australian sheep around the world.

☐ flattened ☐ harbor

B **Complete the sentences.**

entertainment   trade   harbor   increased   flattened   wandered

1 She _______________ her nose against the window.

2 The yacht sailed into the _______________ .

3 The weekly market specializes in the fruit and vegetable _______________ .

4 He _______________ away from the paths to enjoy the peace and quiet of the woods.

5 Your height has _______________ by one centimeter.

6 Everyone enjoyed the _______________ .

What's your favorite type of entertainment?

A **Match to make sentences.**

1 That game gets fantastic reviews, so there's … •   • **a** rays on my skin.

2 Living next to a grocery store is … •   • **b** monitor my scores.

3 Every year, new styles of clothing become … •   • **c** tracker.

4 I want to know if I'm improving, so I … •   • **d** really convenient.

5 I love the feel of the sun's … •   • **e** fashionable.

6 I know how much sleep I get because of my … •   • **f** a lot of demand for it.

B **Read and complete the dialogues.**

fashionable   monitor   rays   convenient   demand   tracker

Sujith: Why are you wearing sunglasses?

Tanya: Because they protect my eyes from the sun's
¹ _______________ . And also because they're
² _______________ !

Yuma: That's a cool watch, Max!

Miguel: Thanks. It isn't just a watch. It's an activity
³ _______________ too. It can ⁴ _______________ my
activity so I know how much exercise I do every day.

Anna: I dream of having a device that can transport me
from one place to another instantly.

Max: Wow! That would be so ⁵ _______________ . I'm
sure there would be a lot of ⁶ _______________ if
someone invented that!

A **Write the infinitive form of these verbs.**

1 were   _______________

2 brought   _______________

3 is raining   _______________

4 have flown   _______________

5 will visit   _______________

6 was sitting   _______________

7 has been lying _______________

8 am   _______________

B **Answer the questions using verb + infinitive.**

1 What did you decide to do yesterday?

____

2 What have you agreed to do that you haven't done yet?

____

3 What famous person do you hope to meet one day?

____

4 What are you planning to do tonight?

____

5 What have you promised to do this week?

____

6 Where do you want to go on vacation next year?

____

C **Write a paragraph about your plans and hopes for the future. Use verb + infinitive and the second conditional.**

I hope to be an astronaut one day. If I was an astronaut, I'd see some amazing places in space! I know it isn't easy to become an astronaut. But I plan to study hard and maybe I'll make my dream come true. Next summer, I want to go to science camp and learn more about space. And my dad has promised to take me to the movie theater on Saturday. He's agreed to see a cool new movie with me, about life on a spaceship. I can't wait!

____

____

____

____

A Read and circle the correct option.

1 There's a lot of [1] **ancestor / agriculture / ray** in my area. There are farms that grow potatoes, and farms that [2] **breed / wander / manufacture** cows. Some farms have chickens, too, and sell eggs at the gate. It's a very [3] **contaminated / fashionable / convenient** way to buy eggs if you don't want to go to a store!

2 About 1,300 years ago, Spain and Portugal were [4] **monitored / flattened / colonized** by people from North Africa and West Asia. The [5] **settlers / harbors / convenience** mostly lived peacefully with the Europeans in the region. They shared their knowledge of math and a [6] **tracker / variety / spice** of sciences. They also did a lot of [7] **trade / demand / entertainment** with the Europeans, selling them food and exotic fabrics.

B Unscramble the words to complete the paragraph.

Making yogurt is a great way to [1] p________________ (pesreevr) fresh milk and keep it edible for longer. Yogurt is also easier to [2] d________________ (gidste) than milk, so some people with an allergy to milk are able to eat yogurt without problems. To make it, you add a little bit of yogurt to warm milk. There is special [3] b________________ (cebairat) in the yogurt. If the milk [4] r________________ (msairen) warm, the number of bacteria in it will [5] i________________ (acereins) and soon the milk will be yogurt.

C Unscramble the sentences.

1 was / I / become / faster / an athlete / would

If I ________________________________ .

2 get / the competition / won / would / if we / a silver cup

We ________________________________ .

3 would / call me / feel upset / didn't / I

If you ________________________________ .

4 would / if / understood / happen / we / animal communication

What ________________________________ ?

5 have fun / if they / in the rain / wouldn't / went / to the beach

They ________________________________ .

Think and Reflect: Unit 14

My understanding of adaptation ☆☆☆☆☆

How well I achieved my goal for Unit 14 ☆☆☆☆☆

The most interesting thing that I learned ________________________________

My goal for Unit 15 ________________________________

How does being adaptable in our thinking help us?

Vocabulary 1

A Circle the correct option.

1 This photographer goes out at **dawn** / **challenge** to get the best pictures.

2 **Challenges** / **Caravans** allow people to go on long trips.

3 This person really enjoys being on a **trapeze** / **measurement** .

4 I love to watch the sun **appear** / **quit** .

5 This carpenter takes **attitudes** / **measurements** before cutting the wood.

6 Some people have a **burn** / **fear** of spiders.

B Read and complete the story.

attitude   quit   challenge   dawn   squash   expected   burn

Nico and Lucas were camping with their dad.

"I don't like camping," said Lucas.

"I don't either," said Nico. They ¹______________ to have a very boring week, so they both had a very grumpy ²______________ . The next day, the boys woke up at ³______________ . As they walked out of the tent, they saw a beautiful view of the mountains.

"This is amazing!" said Nico. Dad nodded in agreement.

"Now for a ⁴______________ !" Dad said "You two boys have to make breakfast on the campfire."

"OK, I'll ⁵______________ some oranges to make juice," said Lucas, "Nico, you cook the sausages, but don't ⁶______________ them!" Very quickly, the boys ⁷______________ feeling grumpy.

A Complete the chart.

telescope geology audible circus auditorium television geometric
circumstance geography circle telecommunication audience

Words with a Latin root that means "hear" or "listen"	Words with a Latin root that means "round"	Words with a Greek root that means "earth"	Words with a Greek root that means "far away"

B Complete the sentences with words from **A**.

1 A _______________ lets you see things that are far away.

2 _______________ is the study of Earth.

3 An _______________ is the part of a theater or hall where the audience sits.

4 Something that is _______________ is something you can hear.

5 A traveling company of entertainers who work in a big tent is called a _______________.

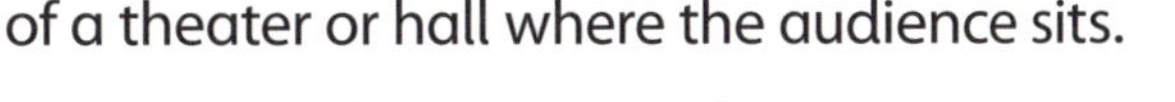

C Find the mistakes in the sentences with sense verbs. Rewrite the sentences correctly.

Chisomo: Hi, Tamara. Are you OK? You looked worriedly in class today.

Tamara: Oh! No, actually I felt ill. I had a headache. The video sounded loudly and it hurt my head. I'm OK now, though.

Chisomo: Great! That's good to know. You look healthily. You also look happy!

Tamara: Thanks. Yes, I feel happily that I can go to the party after school. My mom is making mango ice cream. It tastes so sweetly!

Chisomo: I love mango ice cream! Have fun, Tamara!

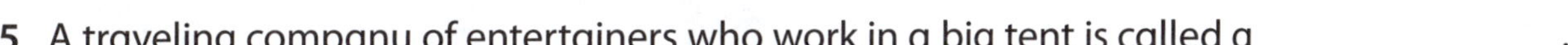

1 You looked worried in class today.

2 ____

3 ____

4 ____

5 ____

1 **A:** How does Tom's new haircut ________________ ?

   B: It ________________ great! It really looks good on him.

2 **A:** How's your dad now? Does he ________________ OK?

   B: No, he still ________________ ill. He has a really bad cold.

3 **A:** Do you ________________ something unpleasant? It ________________ awful in this room.

   B: Uh oh! I forgot to take the trash out!

4 **A:** Does coconut ice cream ________________ salty or sweet?

   B: It ________________ sweet.

5 **A:** How does the band's new song ________________ ?

   B: It ________________ really great. Listen, I'll play it for you now.

E **Decide if the verb is a sense verb. Then check (✓) the correct option.**

1 I ate my lunch ….

   ☐ hungrily   ☐ hungry

2 The sandwich I made tastes very ….

   ☐ saltily   ☐ salty

3 You look … in that new T-shirt.

   ☐ wonderful   ☐ wonderfully

4 Did you see something … in the yard?

   ☐ strange   ☐ strangely

5 The baby rabbit ran … across the grass.

   ☐ quiet   ☐ quietly

6 My favorite band's music sounds ….

   ☐ fantastic   ☐ fantastically

F **Complete the sentences so they're true for you.**

1 I **look** ________________ .

2 I think ________________ **sounds** ________________ .

3 I often **feel** ________________ .

4 In my opinion, ________________ **tastes** ________________ .

5 I think ________________ **smells** ________________ .

Dear Diary ...

4 October, 1936

Wow! It's already four years since I left the Mischka and Moon Traveling Circus and stopped living in my cute little caravan. A lot has changed. Sometimes, I can't believe that now I work as a stuntman* in the movies, but it's true – I do! Mostly, I do stunts that involve high places. I don't have a fear of heights because I worked as a trapeze artist in the circus. I jump out of planes and I climb up buildings! It's a very exciting life.

10 October

The local newspaper interviewed me. Now everyone knows who I am and that I'm a stuntman! It's strange when people just appear in the street and want to take my picture. Today, a group of children saw me and took so many pictures! It made me feel embarrassed. I don't want to be famous. I just love performing tricks. We're going to finish filming the movie this week. I wonder what movie I'll perform in next.

17 December

My last movie finished weeks ago. I'm getting anxious because I don't know when the next movie will be. I hope it's soon; I need to earn some money. Right now, I'm helping out in my local community, working as a tree surgeon. There's a huge oak tree in the park and some of its branches have been slightly broken. It's dangerous, so today, I climbed up the tree and carefully sawed the branches off.

9 January, 1937

It's a new year, but still no new movie! I expect someone will contact me soon. I always keep a positive attitude.

I love new challenges and I like to help people. Last weekend, I volunteered as a firefighter. Going up and down ladders is easy for me. I got the idea of being a firefighter when I saw an old barn burning in a field. I've already done my basic safety training and I start next week.

Glossary:
stuntman = a person (usually in a movie) who performs an exciting action that is dangerous or looks dangerous, instead of an actor

23 January

Firefighting is a tiring job! So far, I've rescued a cat from a rooftop and helped put out three fires. I love the job, but I'm a volunteer, so I don't get paid. I've joined a window-cleaning company to earn some money. As a window cleaner, I get to clean windows way up high! It reminds me of being a trapeze artist and I love it. I miss the circus though. One day, I might go back.

B **Underline these words in the text.**

expect   fear   challenges   appear   caravan   attitude   trapeze   burning

C **Circle the correct option.**

1 Walter **is** / **isn't** afraid of heights.

2 People want to take Walter's picture because he's a **trapeze artist** / **stuntman** .

3 Walter climbed up the huge oak tree to **cut its branches** / **rescue someone** .

4 When Walter saw the barn burning, he decided to **put the fire out** / **become a firefighter** .

5 Walter volunteered to be a **firefighter** / **tree surgeon** .

6 All the jobs Walter did involved **stunts** / **heights** .

D  **What more have you learned about Walter's character from his diary? Read and write *a* or *b*.**

1 Walter is a person who is _______ .

   a brave and not afraid   **b** scared and nervous

2 Walter usually has a _______ .

   a negative attitude   **b** positive attitude

3 Walter is the type of person who _______ .

   a likes to help others   **b** thinks mostly about himself

> **Would you like to do any of the jobs Walter did? Why? / Why not?**

A **Match to make sentences.**

1 I was disappointed because … •
2 My brother and I always sit together … •
3 I make sure I'm on time … •
4 These shoes feel really uncomfortable, … •
5 I always have a bad reaction … •
6 I get frustrated if … •

• **a** for doctors' appointments.
• **b** my cousin couldn't come to stay.
• **c** to this type of medicine.
• **d** I don't understand something.
• **e** probably because my feet have grown.
• **f** in the back of our mom's car.

B **Read and complete the paragraphs.**

> frustrated   disappointed   in the back   on time
> uncomfortable   roadblock   rearrange

On long road trips, my sister and I always play games [1] _______________ of the car.
We [2] _______________ the letters of words to make new words. For example, BAKE and BEAK.
My sister gets very [3] _______________ when she can't make a new word!

My grandmother came with us on our last trip to see my uncle. We left [4] _______________ ,
but after traveling 50 kilometers, there was a [5] _______________ . We got out of the car and saw
hundreds of sheep in the road. There was no way to get through, so we had to go home.

I was [6] _______________ because we couldn't see my uncle. But my grandmother had a more
positive attitude. She could remember the car seats when she was a child. They were made
of wood, and it was very [7] _______________ to sit on them. She felt lucky that she had a nice
modern car to sit in.

A Check (✓) the correct option.

1 Do you … we've been friends for five years already?

☐ innnovative ☐ realize

2 My country's … is trying to improve the lives of its people.

☐ government ☐ pandemic

3 Families who live in different countries often … by phone.

☐ strange ☐ keep in touch

4 I like having … ideas that no one else has had.

☐ innovative ☐ realize

5 A lot of people get ill when there is a ….

☐ pandemic ☐ government

6 I knew there was something wrong with my bike when it made a … noise.

☐ strange ☐ pandemic

B Read and complete the dreams.

innovative   realized   keep in touch   strange   government   pandemic

In my dream, I was an inventor. I had so many [1] _______ ideas! One idea I had was something no one else has ever thought of – a pizza maker that does everything for you!

I had a [2] _______ dream. In my dream, everybody was sneezing. They all had colds because there was a [3] _______ !

I dreamed that the [4] _______ took action to protect every animal on Earth. I thought it was true, but then I [5] _______ I was dreaming.

In my dream, I found a new way to [6] _______ with my friends. I dreamed that my tablet sent my friends pictures of what I had been doing every week.

A Read the memory. Label the different sections.

Final thoughts   Reason for writing   Dialogue

Jacinta

The Week I Was in the Hospital

I chose to write about this week in my life because I made a new best friend. When I was ten years old, I really enjoyed ice skating. One Saturday, I was at my local ice skating rink when I fell over and broke my leg in two places. I spent seven days in the hospital! At first, I was pretty scared about being in the hospital, but I quickly found out that the doctors and nurses were caring and friendly.

On the second morning, I remember waking up and seeing a girl with a broken arm in the bed next to me.

"How are you feeling?" she asked, smiling at me. Her name was Yasmin.

"I'm really bored!" I replied, and we both laughed.

We started chatting about our broken arms and legs and became good friends. I discovered that Yasmin loved skateboarding and swimming. She was also extremely interested in wildlife, just like me! I stopped feeling bored right away. Yasmin taught me how to play chess. I lent her some of my favorite books and we spent hours discussing the plots and characters. Suddenly, being in the hospital didn't seem so bad!

"You look happy," my mom said every day when she came to see me, and I was!

I'll never forget the week I spent in the hospital. My leg is completely mended now and I'm back on the ice, but the best thing about being in the hospital was meeting Yasmin. We message each other most days and we meet up on weekends. Yasmin comes to watch my ice skating shows and I go to her skateboarding competitions. I learned that even when things go a little wrong, something great can happen!

B Answer the questions.

1 Why did Jacinta choose to write about her stay in the hospital?

____

2 How does the dialogue help to tell Jacinta's story?

____

3 How did Jacinta end her memory? Why do you think she did this?

____

C You're going to write a memory of your own. Brainstorm. Write your ideas in the graphic organizer below.

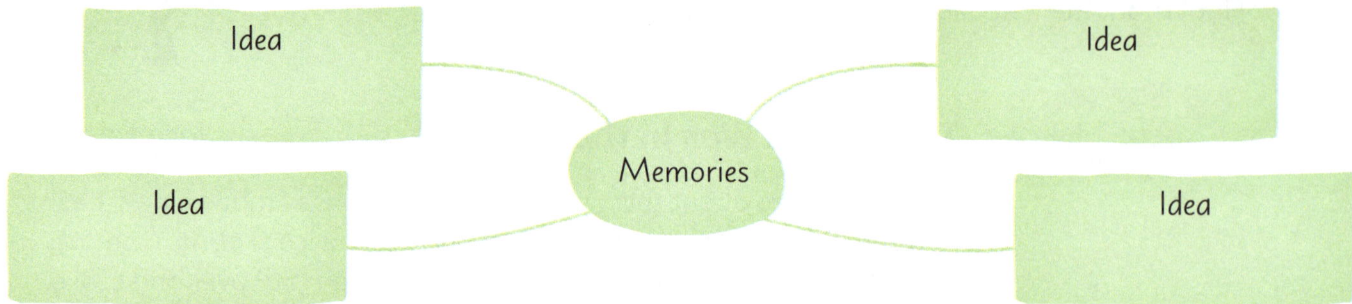

D Choose an idea and plan your memory by completing the chart.

Your memory:	What is your reason for writing about this?
Where and when did this happen?	Can you include some dialogue?
What details can you remember? How did you feel?	What are your final thoughts?

E Now write the first draft of your memory in your notebook.

- Start your memory with your reason for writing about it.
- Say when and where it happened.
- Include some dialogue to make the memory interesting for your readers.
- Write a final paragraph that connects the details in your memory to your reason for writing it.

F Check your work and make any necessary changes.

- Did you do everything in the list in **E**?
- Is your grammar, spelling, and punctuation correct?
- Is your writing clear and easy for other people to understand?

G Now write the final draft of your memory in your notebook. 

A Unscramble the words to complete the paragraphs.

1   Mom made a jacket for me, but it was too small, so I was [1] d_____________ (desadipptoin).
    She thinks she took the wrong [2] m_____________ (suremeemant). Now she says she's going to
    [3] q_____________ (uitq) making clothes.

2   My uncle worked as a [4] t_____________ (zaptree) artist in a circus. He lived in a very cool
    [5] c_____________ (ravacan) and got up to start training at [6] d_____________ (wadn) every day.

3   I like making breakfast for my family. I [7] s_____________ (hsausq) oranges to make
    delicious juice. Unfortunately, I often [8] b_____________ (nubr) the toast, but I enjoy the
    [9] c_____________ (geehallcn)!

B Read and circle the correct option.

I always wear a watch because I like to be [1] **on time / disappointed**. I feel [2] **innovative /
frustrated** and [3] **roadblock / uncomfortable** when other people are late. I told my parents
that we can't go that way because there's a [4] **roadblock / pandemic**. Now they [5] **realize / quit**
why all the cars went the other way. We [6] **rearrange / expect** a traffic officer will come soon.

C Check (✓) the correct option.

1   I love cherries. They … sweet and
    juicy when you bite into them.

    ☐ taste   ☐ tastes

2   What's making that terrible noise?
    It sounds so …!

    ☐ loudly   ☐ loud

3   I'm going to wash my hands. They feel ….

    ☐ dirty   ☐ dirtily

4   Your picture … fantastic! You should
    hang it on the wall.

    ☐ look   ☐ looks

5   The roses we picked smell ….

    ☐ wonderfully   ☐ wonderful

Think and Reflect: Unit 15

My understanding of adaptation ☆☆☆☆☆

How well I achieved my goal for Unit 15 ☆☆☆☆☆

The most interesting thing that I learned ____

My goal for Unit 16 ____

16 What can imagination inspire us to do?

Vocabulary 1

A Complete the sentences.

relaxed   pride   daydream   anger   tumble   trigger

1 His body language showed the _______________ that he was feeling.

2 Watching my mom win her race filled me with _______________ . She rode so well!

3 Doing yoga made me feel very _______________ .

4 My closet is so full that things _______________ out of it if I open the door!

5 These photos _______________ so many memories!

6 Sometimes, when I _______________ in class, I don't do enough work, but I can get fantastic new ideas.

B Check (✓) the correct options. You can check more than one.

1 an antonym of *small*	tiny	big	large
2 a word that's a rhyme for *small*	all	big	ball
3 something that you can gulp	water	a sandwich	jeans
4 something that helps plants to thrive	water	sunlight	pollution
5 a place where something often simmers	on a stove	at a farm	in a yard
6 a reaction when people joke about something	fear	sleep	laughter

A Circle the correct option.

1 This is **your** / **you're** jacket, Diego, but **whose** / **who's** coat is this?

2 **Its** / **It's** a beautiful day. **Where** / **Wear** should we go to enjoy it?

3 **Whose** / **Who's** interested in going to a beach near **here** / **hear** ?

4 **There** / **Their** school has **no** / **know** school uniform.

5 **There** / **Their** are some big waves in the **see** / **sea** today.

6 Can you **here** / **hear** that dog? **Its** / **It's** bark is really loud!

7 I don't **no** / **know** what clothes to **where** / **wear** for the concert.

8 **Your** / **You're** late for school! I can **see** / **sea** the school bus leaving!

9 You ran right **past** / **passed** me yesterday! Did you **here** / **hear** me shout your name?

B Complete the sentences.

> to move   keeping   to take care of   wearing   to sing   meeting

1 Was ________________ a leather jacket fashionable when you were young, Grandpa?

2 ________________ a tiger as a pet is dangerous!

3 Was it sad ________________ away from the place where all your friends lived?

4 It will be embarrassing ________________ in front of everyone's parents at the concert.

5 ________________ my hero was really inspiring.

6 It's important ________________ our planet.

C Match to make sentences.

1 Having a brother who plays drums …   a was fun.

2 Spending all day with my friends …   b is understandable.

3 It was terrifying …   c is noisy.

4 Running a marathon …   d to be so close to that big snake.

5 It will be amusing …   e to be stuck in traffic for so long.

6 It was annoying …   f is difficult.

7 Feeling homesick when you're away from your family …   g to watch that funny show again.

D **Unscramble the sentences.**

1 bike / It / to / without a helmet / safe / wasn't

____

2 a / frustrating / Is / missing / goal / ?

____

3 fascinating / learning / wildlife / about / was / It

____

4 the / Was / puzzle / satisfying / to solve / it / ?

____

E **Rewrite the sentences using the verb forms in parentheses. Don't change the meaning of the sentence.**

1 It's nice to read a book. (gerund)

____

2 It isn't easy to speak Chinese. (gerund)

____

3 Being in a big city was exciting. (infinitive)

____

4 Is it expensive to buy new sneakers? (gerund)

____

5 Was playing table tennis fun? (infinitive)

____

6 Climbing a mountain is tiring. (infinitive)

____

What do you think is fun, exciting, or difficult?

A **Read the poetry blog. What's Aleja's poem about?**

Aleja's Poetry Pages

Say it with a simile!

Today, I've had a lot of fun writing a simile poem. Using similes is useful in poetry, because they help to paint a picture in your reader's mind. You can usually recognize them easily, because they're introduced by the word *as* or *like*.

Posted 3:15 p.m.

Here's an example:

> The boy gulped down his meal as greedily as a hungry wolf.

Does the simile help you to visualize the boy? I have a mental image of someone eating fast, messily, using only his mouth and hands, completely focused on his food.

And here's another example:

> Her anger was like a simmering pot of water.

Here, the simile triggers a mental image of bubbling water. It engages other senses, too: the sound of the bubbles, and how it feels to sit in a bubbly pool. Do you ever feel like that when you're angry? I do! And I also imagine taking off the pot lid, and hot steam flying up into the air. Do you think it's a good way of describing anger?

I decided to make my poem about how it feels to write a poem. It doesn't include any rhymes, but there are a lot of similes.

Finding the Words

My words are like a walk through mud

Heavy steps

Slow

Slippery

My words are like snowflakes in the wind

Dancing

Spinning

Difficult to catch

My words are like a waterfall

Tumbling

Pouring

Unstoppable

My words are like a blue whale's song

Calling

Reaching

Across oceans

Does my poem create any mental images for you? The first verse describes the feeling when I'm staring at an empty page, and the ideas aren't coming very well. In the second verse, the ideas are coming, but they're very disorganized, and some disappear before I can think about them properly. My third verse is about when a lot of words come into my head in a rush, and it's difficult to write them down quickly enough. And my final verse is about how it feels to write on my own, hoping that others will read my poem in my blog, and take notice. The song of a blue whale can travel a thousand kilometers or more, and sometimes another blue whale far, far away replies!

Be like a blue whale and react to my poem with a comment! Or why don't YOU try writing a simile poem? I'd love to see what you write!

B Underline these words in the text.

triggers   anger   simmering   gulped   rhymes   tumbling

C Write the connections that you can make with the text.

Text-to-Self Connections

This part of the text	Made me think about ...

D Answer the questions.

1 What words can a simile start with?

______________ or ______________

2 What three senses are engaged for Aleja by the words *like a simmering pot of water*?

____

3 Which words in Aleja's poem suggest that:

a her ideas aren't coming very well? ______________

b her ideas are disorganized? ______________

c her ideas disappear before she can think about them properly? ______________

d her ideas are coming quickly? ______________

e she wants other people to notice her poem? ______________

What do you think of Aleja's poem? Do you like writing poetry? Why? / Why not?

A Look and write the letter.

a

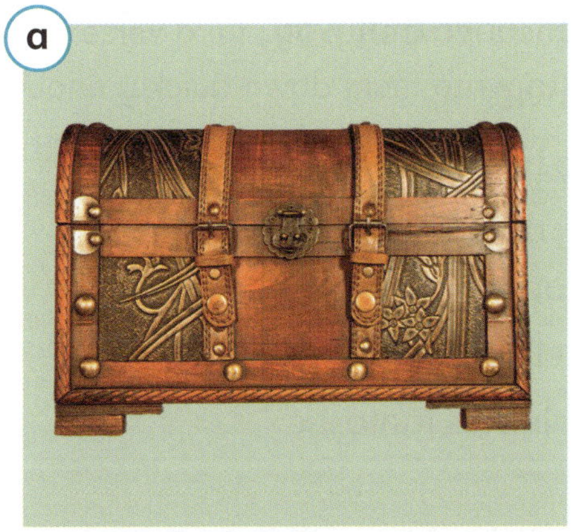

b

c

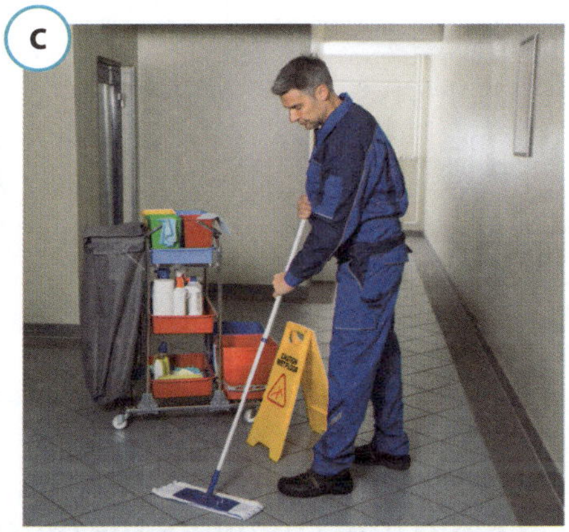

d

e

f

1 The janitor is cleaning the hallway. ______

2 They found a big chest. ______

3 He plays the keyboard. ______

4 There was a big fortress. ______

5 It's a great script. ______

6 He loves to compose music. ______

B Read and circle the correct option.

Our class is performing a show at school next week. We've had a lot to organize. First, we had to decide on a [1]**plot / chest**. It's a mystery about a doctor that disappears! Then, we developed the [2]**props / script**. Different groups wrote the characters' dialogue in different parts of the story. And one group – the most musical people in the class – had to [3]**fortress / compose** some songs.

When all that was done, we organized the characters' costumes, and [4]**props / scripts** such as the doctor's bag and equipment. Luckily, our school [5]**keyboard / janitor** built the scenery for the stage, but he needed help to paint it. And now we're all learning our words and practicing for the performance. It's been hard work, but it's going to be a fantastic show!

A **Match to make sentences.**

1 It's a secret …
2 It's a scene …
3 That's the exit …
4 We're impressed …
5 It's an imaginative …
6 It's a donation …

a so you can leave that way.
b from a movie.
c of $200 to help the animal shelter.
d idea, very different from what's usually done.
e so don't tell anyone.
f and we think it's fantastic.

B **Read and complete the paragraph.**

donation   scene   imaginative   exit   impressed   secret

This semester, I've been going to a technology club every Saturday. I'm really ¹_______________ with it – the teachers are great! At the moment, we're designing video games. I'm really ²_______________, so I have a lot of exciting ideas for my game. In the first ³_______________, a wildlife park receives a ⁴_______________ of a mysterious animal. For the rest of the game, you have to look after the animal. If you don't feed it enough, it dies. If you don't block every ⁵_______________ from its living area, it escapes. And if you don't keep it a ⁶_______________ from the park's visitors, bad people find out about it. Then they come at night and take it away. Creating all the different parts of the game won't be easy, but I think it's going to be cool!

A **Circle the correct option.**

1 **Do** / **Does** anyone want to perform in a show?

2 Everyone in my school **has written** / **have written** a poem.

3 All my friends **like** / **likes** wearing bracelets.

4 A bug hotel is easy to make, and it really **help** / **helps** insects.

5 Nobody in my class **want** / **wants** to compose songs.

6 My brothers are learning to play the keyboard. They **is getting** / **are getting** very good at it.

B **Rewrite the sentences so they have a similar meaning. Use the words in parentheses.**

1 All of us love vacations. (everyone)

Everyone loves vacations.

2 Does anybody live there? (people)

3 They all play badminton. (all of them)

4 You and I are lucky. (we)

5 People don't care about it. (nobody)

6 Do any of you want my help? (anybody)

C **Write a paragraph about your creative heroes. Use the correct pronoun agreement.**

I have many heroes who are very creative. My musical heroes are the four people in my favorite band, Dzokpo. No one is better than them at composing and performing songs, and they are also great dancers. I go to dance classes, but it isn't easy to dance as well as Dzokpo! I love street art, and I have a hero who's a street artist named Street Doctor. Everyone in my city thinks her murals are really cool. Finally, I love reading stories, and one of my heroes is the writer Kofi Konadu. His stories are set in many different African countries and I love to learn about life in these interesting places.

A **Unscramble the words to complete the paragraph.**

My job is to write funny movie [1] s____________ (pticrss). It's the perfect job for me because I've always loved to [2] j____________ (ekjo) with my friends and family, and I've always been [3] i____________ (miegavintai) and creative. I often [4] d____________ (yadmeard) about funny situations that people might get into. It's fun to develop a [5] p____________ (tpol) for a movie with an amusing situation in every [6] s____________ (encse). I get stressed when a movie company needs a script very urgently, but I [7] t____________ (hritev) as a writer when there's more time and I feel more [8] r____________ (xdealre). I take a lot of [9] p____________ (dpier) in my work. Making people laugh is the best job in the world!

B **Circle the correct option.**

1   In the game, you have to attack your enemy's **fortress** / **donation** / **gulp** and try to get inside it.

2   It isn't a real robot. It's a **chest** / **prop** / **rhyme** for a movie.

3   *Hard* is an **exit** / **anger** / **antonym** of *soft*, and also of *easy*.

4   There's a problem with the faucet. Let's get the **trigger** / **simmer** / **janitor**.

C **Complete the sentences with the correct form of the verbs.**

give   ride   punish   invent   remember

1   It isn't easy ____________ everyone's names when you join a new class.

2   ____________ a camel isn't very comfortable.

3   It was very generous of you ____________ such an expensive present.

4   It's unfair ____________ me, because I didn't do anything wrong.

5   ____________ characters for a story is fun.

Think and Reflect: Unit 16

My understanding of imagination ☆☆☆☆☆

How well I achieved my goal for Unit 16 ☆☆☆☆☆

The most interesting thing that I learned ____________________

My goal for Unit 17 ____________________

Vocabulary 1

A **Complete the sentences.**   cabin   pose   embarrassed   artistic   experiment   engineering

1 We spend our winter vacation in this ______________ in the woods.

2 Lydia is a very ______________ person.

3 The boy was ______________ because he broke the window.

4 Our teacher showed us how to ______________ with different chemicals.

5 In this game you have to hold a ______________ like this for as long as you can.

6 This bridge in Japan is an amazing example of ______________ .

B **Read and circle the correct option.**

When I was very young, I was [1]**shy** / **session** . I didn't really enjoy speaking in class or meeting new people. But I always had an [2]**inventive** / **ambition** to be an actor in a play. Last Saturday, I decided to go to my local theater. They have special [3]**sessions** / **explanations** every week for children who want to give acting a try. At first, I wasn't sure what I had to do, but I met several children who gave me good advice and [4]**explanations** / **cabins** . The best part was trying on different costumes. Most of them didn't [5]**pose** / **fit** me because they were too big, but I found one that was perfect! I also really enjoyed playing different characters because I had the opportunity to be [6]**shy** / **inventive** .

A **Complete the chart.**

> attract   impressive   create   act   collaborative   protect   cooperative
> collaborate   creative   attractive   cooperate   impress   protective   active

Verbs	Adjectives

B **Complete the sentences with verbs or adjectives from A.**

1 Look at that fox. It wants to _______________ its babies.

2 I'm going to _______________ my friends by solving this difficult math puzzle.

3 My brother has fantastic ideas; he's very _______________.

4 These gorgeous flowers always _______________ the bees.

5 I love to move around; I'm very _______________.

6 Let's work together. It's fun to be _______________.

7 I don't want to argue with you. If we both _______________, we will be able to finish the project on time.

C **Circle the correct option.**

1 Do you want to make **a** / **an** / **–** origami model with me?

2 **The** / **A** / **An** model I want to make is a rocket.

3 The rocket will have **an** / **the** / **–** engine and **a** / **an** / **the** telescope.

4 Astronauts have a lot of space inside to eat **the** / **–** / **a** dinner and go to sleep.

5 One day, I hope my rocket will take off from **an** / **the** / **–** Australia.

6 It won't use gas, so it will be good for **an** / **–** / **the** environment.

7 I like to play **a** / **the** / **–** games with my models.

1 Marco lives in the United Kingdom.

2 He enjoys playing basketball and learning about science.

3 Would you like apple for your snack?

4 The apple I picked from the tree was delicious!

5 Is that elephant or a mammoth?

6 It's not a mammoth. Mammoths are extinct.

E Find the mistakes. Rewrite the sentences with the correct articles.

1 I'm going to the kitchen. Do you need anything from a refrigerator?

I'm going to the kitchen. Do you need anything from the refrigerator?

2 Oh, yes, please. I'd like an piece of cheese.

3 Next month, we're going on vacation to the Peru.

4 That's great! We learned about that country in a geography.

5 I'm playing the baseball with my friends on Saturday.

6 Cool. I'm going to see a movie I told you about yesterday.

F Complete the missing articles. If no article is needed, write –.

1 _______________ poem in Unit 16 is about _______________ starfish.

2 _______________ starfish is small and orange. It's named *Little Orange Starfish*.

3 There's _______________ place in Zanzibar that's famous for starfish.

4 Zanzibar is _______________ island off the coast of _______________ Tanzania.

5 I love wildlife, so when I go to college, I hope to study _______________ zoology.

A **Read the reviews. Which game is only played online?**

Great Games to Trigger the Imagination!

Funny Story Dice ★★★★★ Max

Do you have an ambition to be a great storyteller? Buy this game to improve your skills! Here's how a storytelling session goes.

Inside the box, you'll find six dice. On each side of the dice, there's a picture. Take turns to throw the dice. Look at the pictures and begin telling your story, using each picture in turn to help you. I recommend this game for anyone who loves stories.

> "One night, when the moon and stars were shining, it began to rain hard! It rained until the whole town filled with water. I saw cars floating by. I was swimming down the street when a whale came and rescued me …"

Charades ★★★ Katriona

I just played this for the first time! It's a fantastic game for anyone who feels shy or embarrassed because it makes everyone laugh. It's very simple, too. Just write the titles of movies, books, or songs that you know on pieces of paper. Players take turns to take one title out of the box and act it out. You can't use any words—only actions! The other players have to guess the title. I give it three stars because sometimes it's hard to guess titles that you don't know well.

WorldZone ★★★★★ Charlie

This is an amazing online game that all inventive children should try. Here's a quick explanation. Using your imagination, you can build almost anything you like. I'm interested in engineering, so I chose to build a skyscraper made from stone and gold! I found all the materials I needed. Then, I used gray and white stone blocks to build the base of the building and all 20 stories. Next, I put in some windows. I had to dig for gold, but I got it! Finally, I covered the whole skyscraper in gold. It was awesome!

B Underline these words in the text.

embarrassed   session   explanation   ambition   inventive   shy   engineering

C Scan the four reviews to find the answers.

1 the number of dice in Max's game   ______________________

2 types of titles that you can act out in Charades   ______________________

3 the materials that Charlie used for his skyscraper   ______________________

4 two things that FixIt encourages you to be   ______________________

D Check (✓) the correct option.

1 Which game uses pictures?
- [ ] Charades
- [ ] Funny Story Dice

2 Charades is a good game for ….
- [ ] inventive children
- [ ] children who are shy

3 Who is interested in engineering?
- [ ] Charlie
- [ ] Zak

4 How does Charlie find gold?
- [ ] by guessing
- [ ] by digging

5 Which game is set on a fantasy island?
- [ ] FixIt
- [ ] Funny Story Dice

6 Which game involves role-playing?
- [ ] FixIt
- [ ] Charades

What's your favorite game? Why do you like it?

A Match to make sentences.

1 If you separate something, …
2 If you use an aid, …
3 If you make a moment memorable, …
4 If you see someone occasionally, …
5 If you're unable to catch the bus, …
6 If you find math tricky, …

a you might find things easier.
b it might take you longer to figure it out.
c you might have to walk.
d you'll have two things instead of one.
e you might not recognize them right away.
f people will remember it.

B Complete the sentences.

unable   tricky   aid   place   chunk   memorable

1 Let's _______________ the beautiful flowers on the table.

2 It's sometimes _______________ making toast because it burns!

3 Could I please have a small _______________ of cheese?

4 He's _______________ to swim, but he wants to learn.

5 I won't forget that view. It was very _______________ .

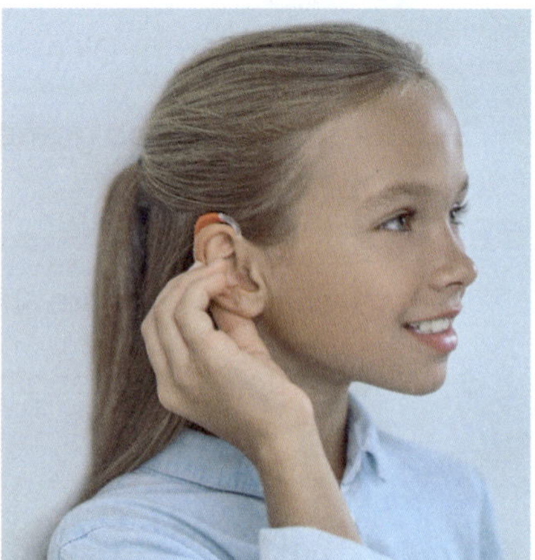

6 Maria uses an _______________ to help her hear better.

A Check (✓) the correct option.

1 I am very … in all sports. I love to win!

☐ weakness ☐ pressure ☐ competitive

2 I have … to compete in the Olympic Games when I'm an adult.

☐ set a goal ☐ competitive ☐ weakness

3 My family give me a lot of …!

☐ weakness ☐ immediately ☐ motivation

4 My ankle is my only ….

☐ motivation ☐ pressure ☐ weakness

5 Sometimes, there's a lot of … when everyone is watching.

☐ competitive ☐ pressure ☐ immediately

6 Of course, I fall down, but I get up …!

☐ set a goal ☐ motivation ☐ immediately

B Read and complete the dialogue.

weakness   pressure   competitive   motivation   set a goal   immediately

Juan: Are you a [1] _______________ person, Tom? Do you like to be first in everything?

Tom: I enjoy doing things well, but I don't enjoy feeling [2] _______________ . How about you?

Juan: Oh, yes! I have a lot of [3] _______________ to do my best for the team.

Tom: I'd like to be on the swim team, but I have some [4] _______________ in my arms.
This year, I've [5] _______________ to swim 10 kilometers a month. That should help.

Juan: Cool! That's a great thing to try to do. When do you start?

Tom: [6] _______________ ! In fact, I'm going to the pool now. Join me!

A Write *Sentence* or *Fragment*. Correct the fragments.

1 I'd like to recycle more plastic. _______________
Going to save yogurt pots. _______________

____

2 Many groups working hard. _______________
They're trying to stop plastic pollution. _______________

____

3 Turtles killed by plastic trash. _______________
Many fish and dolphins face the same problem. _______________

____

4 My friends are raising funds for wildlife protection. _______________
Want to join them. _______________

____

B How many fragments are there? Read and circle the answer.

Tigers still in some parts of India. Unfortunately, they are endangered even now. I'd like to help save the tigers. Beautiful animals! Going to write letters. I think that it's important to take action to protect these animals. I don't want them to become extinct. Under threat in their habitat.

1 / 2 / 3 / 4

C Write a paragraph on a topic you care about. Use full sentences.

This month, we've learned a lot about how to use our memory better. That's a topic that I find interesting. I enjoyed finding out how to remember numbers. You can break long numbers into chunks. That makes it a lot easier to remember phone numbers, for example. I have also practiced the memory palace technique when I want to remember a list of things. It's fun!

____

____

____

____

____

A Read and circle the correct option.

Winning events in sports is a big [1] **motivation** / **explanation** / **chunk** for many athletes. Sportspeople all over the world are very [2] **shy** / **competitive** / **embarrassed** and spend many years working under [3] **session** / **pose** / **pressure**. They all want to achieve their [4] **ambitions** / **cabins** / **aids**. Many athletes like to [5] **set goals** / **place** / **separate** every year. Good sportspeople know their own [6] **explanations** / **poses** / **weaknesses** and work hard to overcome them. Of course, it's often [7] **memorable** / **tricky** / **immediately** to win in big competitions such as the Olympics because there are many talented people. However, most athletes start a set of training [8] **chunks** / **poses** / **sessions** believing that they can achieve great things!

B Check (✓) the correct option.

1 We slept in a … in the woods.

☐ cabin   ☐ chunk

2 My … is to learn to play the drums.

☐ pressure   ☐ ambition

3 It was a … day. In fact I'll never forget it!

☐ memorable   ☐ embarrassed

4 I don't understand how this game works. I need an … .

☐ aid   ☐ explanation

C Complete the sentences with *a*, *an*, *the*, or – (no article).

Did you see [1] ________ sunset this evening? It was [2] ________ incredible color! I watched it set while I was eating [3] ________ dinner. The whole sky looked orange because of the reflections from [4] ________ sun. I remember seeing another sunset like this one when I lived in [5] ________ South Africa. I wish I was [6] ________ artist. That way I'd be able to capture the sunset in [7] ________ painting! Maybe if I work hard at [8] ________ art in school, I might achieve my ambition.

Think and Reflect: Unit 17

My understanding of imagination ☆☆☆☆☆

How well I achieved my goal for Unit 17 ☆☆☆☆☆

The most interesting thing that I learned ________________________________

My goal for Unit 18 ________________________________

Vocabulary 1

A **Read and circle the correct option.**

There's a business in my town that manufactures leather shoes. Some are [1] **senior / ordinary** shoes that everyone wears, but others are very unusual, for performers in movies and theater shows. It's a very [2] **junior / successful** business, with a lot of happy customers all over the world. My aunt is a [3] **fed up / senior** manager there. She's in charge of the factory, and my big brother works for her. My aunt loves her job, but my brother's a little [4] **fed up / ordinary** with his. He monitors the machines that cut the leather and [5] **punch / principle** holes in it. He's learning the [6] **punches / principles** of factory production, but it's a [7] **junior / successful** job, and he wants more responsibility.

B **Read and complete the dialogue.**

> explode   reality   grin   asteroids   confirm

Asaf: Do big rocks from space sometimes hit planet Earth in [1] ________________ , or does this just happen in the movies?

Zeynep: It can happen in the real world, too. The big rocks are called [2] ________________ .

Asaf: Are they really dangerous?

Zeynep: Not usually. They almost always [3] ________________ into tiny fragments when they enter Earth's atmosphere, and they don't do much damage. But very occasionally – maybe four times in a million years – a big asteroid is still in one piece when it hits Earth, and the impact is terrifying.

Asaf: What happens?

Zeynep: Well, when a huge asteroid hit Mexico 66 million years ago, it caused problems for the whole planet. Scientists can't [4] ________________ this, but they think the dinosaurs went extinct because of it!

Asaf: Hey, don't [5] ________________ ! You shouldn't smile about dinosaurs dying.

Zeynep: I know it's sad. But it's kind of awesome to imagine the power of an asteroid like that!

A **Complete the sentences. Use the same word in both blanks, and write *Noun* or *Verb*.**

notice   picture   watch   cook   ~~work~~   project   shelter   kick

1 My parents _____work_____ (*Verb*) hard all week, but they don't do any _____work_____ (noun) on the weekends.

2 I hate this rain! There's a bus _______________ (_____) over there. Let's _______________ (_____) under it until the rain stops.

3 There's a new _______________ (_____) telling us not to walk on the grass. Did you _______________ (_____) it?

4 Now _______________ (_____) the ball to Lilato. That was a great _______________ (_____)!

5 My school _______________ (_____) was about the history of movies. I used old movie equipment to _______________ (_____) a scene from an old movie onto the classroom wall.

6 My dad's a really good _______________ (_____), but my mom can only _______________ (_____) eggs and toast.

7 Do you like my new _______________ (_____)? It doesn't just tell the time. It has an Internet connection too, and you can _______________ (_____) TV shows on it!

8 In art today, you're going to draw a _______________ (_____) that shows your future. First, close your eyes and imagine your future life. What do you _______________ (_____)?

B **Read and circle the correct option.**

1 **A:** It's time for bed now, Blanca.

B: Please can I have five more minutes? I **play** / **'m playing** a cool video game and I **'ve come** / **'ve been coming** to the most exciting part.

2 **A:** Why are your clothes dirty?

B: I **'ve planted** / **'ve been planting** flowers in the backyard. The flowers **will make** / **were making** our local bees happy this summer!

3 **A:** Where were you at four o'clock?

B: I **walked** / **was walking** home from school with Abdul. I **got** / **was getting** home at about 4:30.

4 **A:** What are your plans for the summer?

B: I **'ll stay** / **'m going to stay** at my grandparents' farm. I **go** / **'m going** there every year. They **collect** / **'re collecting** me from my house next Tuesday.

C **Correct the mistakes with the underlined verbs.**

1   My brother <u>go</u> to a science club every Monday.

2   We <u>going to design</u> a rocket in class next week.

3   They <u>didn't went</u> to school yesterday because they were ill.

4   My sister <u>will to be</u> five years old next month.

5   I <u>have being reading</u> science-fiction stories this week.

6   <u>I've never saw</u> a spaceship.

D **Complete the sentences with the correct form of the verbs in parentheses.**

1   Last Sunday, my mom ________________________ (wash) our car.

2   I ________________________ (watch) this TV show for an hour, and it hasn't finished yet.

3   We've been planning a cycle route for next weekend. We ________________________ (ride) to a beautiful waterfall.

4   I never wake up early, so I probably ________________________ (wake up) early tomorrow.

5   So far this month, I ________________________ (read) three books.

6   I ________________________ (meet) my friends at the park this afternoon. I can't wait!

E **Read and complete. Use the correct form of the verbs and each of the tenses or future forms once.**

spread   teach   visit   ~~become~~   help   develop   remember   work

simple present   present continuous   ~~simple past~~   past continuous
present perfect   present perfect continuous   *will*   *going to*

Kizzmekia Corbett loved studying science in school, and after university she ¹________became________ a scientist. Since then, her research ²________________________ the whole world. In 2020, a dangerous disease called Covid-19 ³________________________ all over the planet, and no one knew how to protect people from it. Kizzmekia and her team developed a Covid-19 vaccine that saved many lives. Future generations ⁴________________________ Kizzmekia's life-saving work for a long time.

Kizzmekia still ⁵________________________ as a scientist. At the moment, she ⁶________________________ a vaccine for another dangerous disease. But she is also an educator. For the last few years, she ⁷________________________ people about how useful and safe vaccines are. And next Tuesday, she ⁸________________________ our school! We can't wait to meet her.

What have you been doing today? What are you going to do tomorrow?

Up, Up, and Away!

Junior scientists Chaiya and Jittra were on their way to another TV studio. These days, everyone seemed to want to interview them about how they saved planet Earth with their asteroid-punching rocket.

"Up, up, and away!" said Jittra as the elevator rushed them to the 49th floor.

"This elevator's traveling so fast, it's like being in a rocket!" said Chaiya.

Soon, the interview started. Chaiya and Jittra were asked about the asteroid-punching rocket, and then about their ambitions for the future.

"We want to think of more ideas that will change the world!" said Chaiya.

"And we've always dreamed of having a vacation in space!" added Jittra.

"Maybe you'll be able to do that soon," said the interviewer.

"I don't know," said Chaiya. "Planes and cars have been using too much fossil fuel, and rockets use even more. Imagine the problems for the environment if everyone had vacations in space!"

"That could be your next project," suggested the interviewer. "Space travel that doesn't use fossil fuel."

After the interview, Chaiya and Jittra took the elevator down to street level.

"Could we travel into space in an elevator?" asked Chaiya. "Like an ordinary elevator, but much taller?"

"I don't think we could design a building tall enough to support the elevator," said Jittra.

They walked past some athletes. One was spinning a heavy metal ball on the end of a chain, then throwing it as far as he could.

"Hey!" said Jittra excitedly. "When the ball and chain are spun, they don't hang down vertically. They fly out horizontally, as far away from the athlete as possible. And think! Earth is spinning in space, just like the athlete."

"Oh! I see!" said Chaiya. "So a space elevator could follow the same principle as the ball and chain. As Earth spins, the top end of the elevator would stay as far from Earth as possible – right up in space!"

They rushed to their workplace, Science Solutions Lab, and did some calculations. "I think this is going to work!" grinned Jittra.

Two years later, their project was finished. The world's first space elevator used solar power, and extended 42,000 km above Earth's surface.

Chaiya and Jittra got into the elevator and pressed the button.

"Up, up, and away!" they said, as buildings, cities, and oceans got smaller and smaller. They were heading into space!

B **Underline these words in the text.**

junior   asteroid   grinned   punching   principle   ordinary

C **Complete the sentences.**

1 Chaiya and Jittra take an elevator to the 49th floor to go _____________________.

2 Chaiya thinks the elevator is similar to _____________________.

3 The TV interviewer thinks that Chaiya and Jittra should invent _____________________.

4 Jittra gets her idea for the space elevator design from _____________________ on the end of a chain.

5 The space elevator uses _____________________.

D **Answer the questions by drawing your own conclusions.**

1 Have Chaiya and Jittra given TV interviews before?

____

2 During the interview, how does Chaiya feel about a future where everyone goes to space on vacation? Why?

____

3 What do Chaiya and Jittra think of the interviewer's suggestion for their next project?

____

4 How long do you think Chaiya and Jittra will be in space? Why?

____

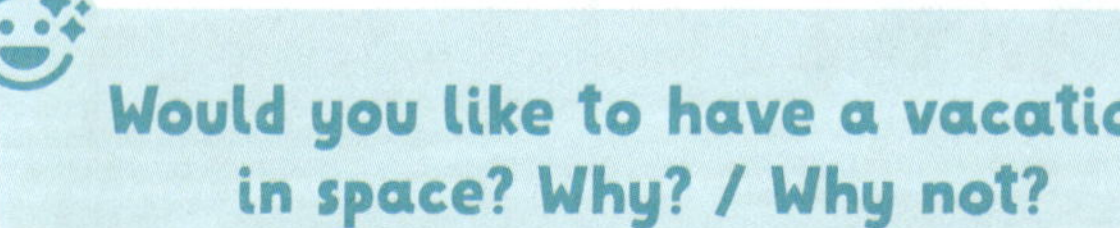

A Match to make sentences.

1 You need to update …
2 Farmers harvest …
3 When cars kill …
4 It's a very steep …
5 The building must be accessible …
6 The door is transparent …

a walk from the beach to the top of the cliff.
b your computer, because it's very old.
c corn so people can eat it.
d so you can see through it.
e to people in wheelchairs.
f animals on the roads, it's very sad.

B Read and circle the correct option.

On Saturday, the weather was very [1] **pleasant** / **transparent**, so we decided to enjoy the sunshine and go for a walk. First, we took a [2] **kill** / **steep** path up a hill. We wanted to get to the viewpoint at the top, but unfortunately the top part of the path wasn't [3] **accessible** / **steep**. There were a lot of vines growing across it, blocking our way. We turned back and took a different path, next to a river. I enjoyed looking at the insects flying above the water. Their delicate wings were as [4] **accessible** / **transparent** as glass! Later, we went

past a yard full of beautiful sunflowers. We chatted to the woman who lived there. She's going to [5] **harvest** / **update** the sunflower seeds in the fall and make oil with them. Making your own oil from plants that you've grown would be such a cool [6] **harvest** / **achievement**! I'd love to try it one day.

A Check (✓) the correct option.

1 You … me when you give me too many instructions at once.

☐ suffer   ☐ confuse

2 The … says that you can't drive a car in this country until you're 18.

☐ law   ☐ echolocation

3 When there's bad air pollution, humans and animals … .

☐ suffer   ☐ confuse

4 If something metal is left in a fire for a long time, it turns red and … .

☐ glows   ☐ issues

5 Animals need a good sense of hearing to navigate by … .

☐ law   ☐ echolocation

6 Climate change is a big … , and we need to do all that we can to stop it.

☐ glow   ☐ issue

B Read and complete the paragraph.

law   echolocation   glows   issues   suffer   confuse

Unfortunately, there are many [1]_______________ in the world that make people and animals [2]_______________. But with imagination, we can solve many problems! For example, one group of inventors imagined a blind person who had the navigation skills of a bat. The inventors designed a walking stick that uses [3]_______________ to identify obstacles in the blind person's path and guides the person to avoid them. Another group imagined a city that didn't need electric lights at night. They designed paint for road signs that can [4]_______________ in the dark. And a government imagined how a new [5]_______________ to stop pollution from cars might affect people with different jobs and ways of life. They made sure that the law was fair to everyone, and clear enough that it didn't [6]_______________ anyone.

A **Read the science-fiction story. Label the sections that answer the questions.**

Who? What? When? Where? Why?

A Day with Dinosaurs

Suyin was a scientist with one important question to answer: could her favorite dinosaurs, microraptors, fly?

She packed a bag with her holographic camera and some snacks. Then she got inside her new invention, the TimeTripper machine, and moved the lever to the left. Immediately, she felt the machine start to spin. When the spinning stopped, she was in the year 120 million BCE!

She walked through a beautiful land of extinct plants and animals. But a huge gray dinosaur smelled the snacks in her bag. It picked up the bag with its teeth and Suyin went flying. Soon she and the bag were stuck around the dinosaur's neck. *Oh no!* she thought. *How can I escape? I'm too high to jump.*

She took her Sonic Supercutters from her pocket. When the dinosaur went past a tree, she cut through the strap of her bag. She and the bag fell onto a tree branch, and the dinosaur continued on its way.

She crawled along the branch until she came to a big pile of sticks. It was a nest! And there were some cute baby dinosaurs in it, with fluffy dark feathers on their four little legs. She couldn't identify their species – baby dinosaurs looked very different from their parents.

As she started to film the baby dinosaurs, their mother flew toward the nest. She was a microraptor! She circled above them on her dark wings. *Everyone will accept that microraptors can fly now,* thought Suyin as she filmed the mother dinosaur. She just had to figure out how to get home …

B **Answer the questions.**

1 Who is the character?

2 Why does she go on a journey?

3 When and where is most of the story set?

4 What problem does she have?

C You're going to write a science-fiction story about a journey. Brainstorm.
Write your ideas in the graphic organizer below.

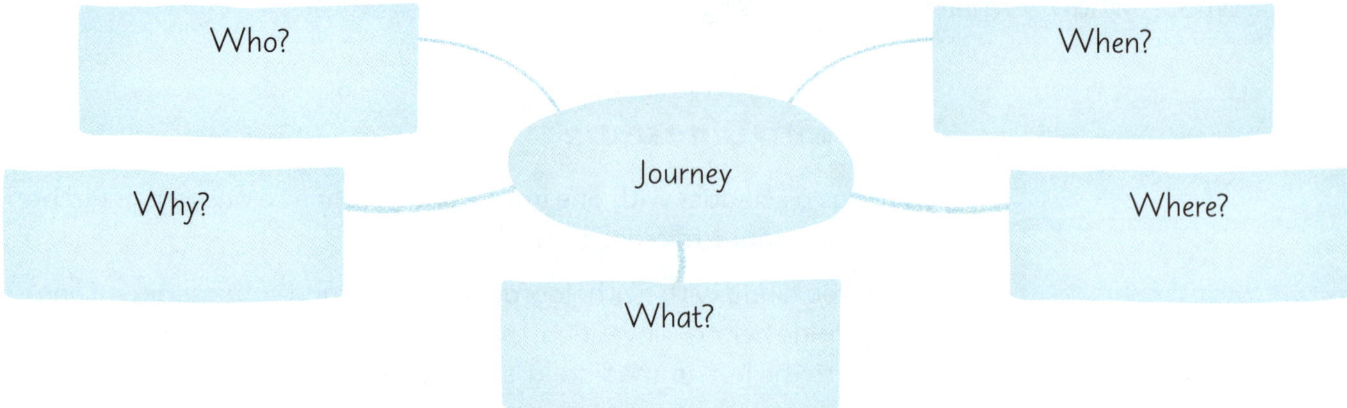

D Outline your ideas by completing the chart.

Character(s):

Setting (time and place):

Reason for the journey:

Problem in the story:

How the problem is solved:

Ending:

E Now write the first draft of your story in your notebook.

- Include one or more interesting characters. You want your readers to care about what happens to them.
- Describe where and when the story takes place. You want your readers to be able to visualize the setting.
- Include a problem for the characters, which causes events to happen.
- Make the characters solve the problem at the end of the story.

F Check your work and make any necessary changes.

- Did you do everything in the list in **E**?
- Is your grammar, spelling, and punctuation correct?
- Is your writing clear and easy for other people to understand?

G Now write the final draft of your story in your notebook.

A **Unscramble the words to complete the paragraph.**

And next in the news, we can [1] u_____________ (detapu) you on the latest mission to Mars. We can
[2] c_____________ (mricnof) that three astronauts have successfully landed their spaceship on
the planet. What a fantastic [3] a_____________ (evahcmtneie)! The dream of landing on Mars has
become a [4] r_____________ (aryelti)!

B **Read and circle the correct option.**

I'm [1] **junior / fed up / accessible** with reading this book, *Asteroid Attack*. I expected it to be
an exciting science-fiction story, but in [2] **reality / grin / principle**, it's about [3] **suffer / issue /
ordinary** people in a boring town, and I don't find it very interesting. My ambition is to
be a [4] **harvest / steep / successful** writer when I'm older. But I'd also like to be a [5] **senior /
transparent / confuse** police officer. It would be cool to be responsible for protecting my
city from people who don't follow the [6] **achievement / law / echolocation**.

C **Unscramble the sentences and write the correct tense.**

simple present   present continuous   simple past
past continuous   present perfect   present perfect continuous

1 hours / been / have / sleeping / for / You

_______________________________   _______________________________

2 nice / him / a / We / gift / gave

_______________________________   _______________________________

3 tennis / always / I / on / play / Saturdays

_______________________________   _______________________________

4 have / We / photos / a lot / taken / of

_______________________________   _______________________________

5 the / studying / at / Everyone / moment / is

_______________________________   _______________________________

6 was / all day / It / yesterday / raining

_______________________________   _______________________________

Think and Reflect: Unit 18

My understanding of imagination ☆☆☆☆☆

How well I achieved my goal for Unit 18 ☆☆☆☆☆

The most interesting thing that I learned ____

Descriptive Essay

A Read the descriptive essay. Label the different sections.

Personal connection   Introduction   Description

My Favorite View

There are many beautiful views on our planet, both in cities and in the natural world. Like many other people, I have traveled a long way to see famous views, for example of castles, skyscrapers, and waterfalls. My favorite view, however, is just a short walk from my home, at a place called Weatherdown Forest.

I love the view from my favorite bench in the forest at all times of year. In the summer, sun streams through the gaps between the tall trees and fills the forest with light. In the fall, the forest leaves change from green into wonderful bright reds, oranges, and yellows. And in the winter, snow decorates the trees and covers the ground in a smooth white blanket. However, my favorite view only exists for three weeks every spring. In those three weeks, the forest floor is covered in wonderful bluebell flowers. In my opinion, there is nothing as beautiful as the deep blue of those flowers next to the pale green of spring leaves.

Weatherdown Forest has been special to me since I was very young. It makes me feel part of nature and the changing seasons. And when the first bluebells arrive in the spring, it feels like a sign of hope for the future. When something is so beautiful, it's impossible to believe that bad things might happen in the world.

B Answer the questions.

1 How does the writer introduce their descriptive essay?

____

2 What exactly is the writer's favorite view?

____

3 What is their personal connection with the view?

____

C **You're going to write a descriptive essay about your favorite view. Brainstorm. Write your ideas in the graphic organizer below.**

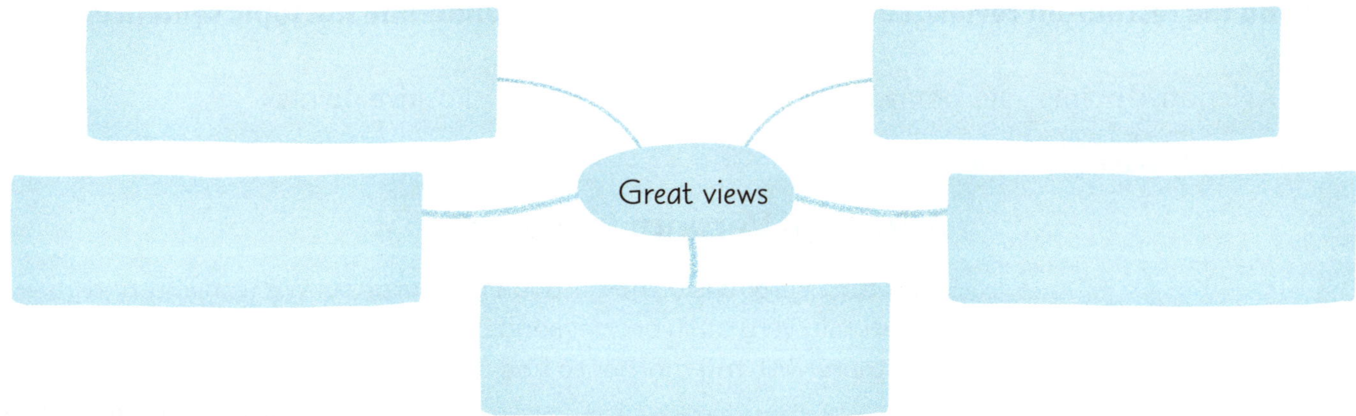

D **Outline your ideas by completing the chart.**

Favorite view:	
Description:	**Personal connection:**

E **Now write the first draft of your descriptive essay in your notebook.** 

- Start your descriptive essay with some background information, and introduce the view that you are writing about.
- Describe exactly what you can see.
- Use adjectives in the correct order.
- Say when the view looks most interesting.
- Explain why this view is special to you, and how it makes you feel.

F **Check your work and make any necessary changes.**

- Did you do everything in the list in **E**?
- Is your grammar, spelling, and punctuation correct?
- Is your writing clear and easy for other people to understand?

G **Now write the final draft of your descriptive essay in your notebook.**

Review

A Read the restaurant review. Label the different sections. Underline the topic sentences.

Negative points   Recommendation   Short description   Positive points

A Taste of Verona: A Review

A Taste of Verona is a small Italian restaurant in Wentonville, and it is usually very busy on weekends. Is it as great as people say? I ate there with my mother to find out.

There was plenty that we liked. My pizza looked attractive and tasted delicious, and I particularly appreciated its generous layer of cheese. My mother had seafood pasta and she said that it had a lot of flavor. Our desserts – a mouth-watering lemon cake with juicy strawberries, and a tasty chocolate ice cream – were also great. The prices were lower than in other local restaurants, and the colorful pictures on the restaurant walls gave the place a lively atmosphere.

However, we were disappointed by two things. First, the servers kept asking customers to eat more quickly because the restaurant was so busy! I definitely prefer restaurants with servers who are more patient and friendly. Second, our table was dirty. We had to ask three times for someone to clean it.

In general, I recommend A Taste of Verona if you like Italian food, but suggest that you try to go there on a quiet day. When the restaurant is very busy, the servers may stop you from relaxing and enjoying your meal.

B Answer the questions.

1 How does the writer begin the review?

____

2 What positive and negative points does the writer make?

Positive: _______________________________________

Negative: _______________________________________

3 How does the writer end the review?

____

C **You're going to write a review. Brainstorm. Write your ideas in the graphic organizer below.**

D **Do some research and outline your ideas by completing the chart.**

A review of:	
Short description:	
Positive points:	**Negative points:**
Recommendation:	

E **Now write the first draft of your review in your notebook.**

- Give a short description of the thing that you are reviewing.
- Describe your own experience.
- Include both positive and negative points, in separate paragraphs.
- Use topic sentences to introduce the positive and negative points.
- Finish with your general feeling, and a recommendation.

F **Check your work and make any necessary changes.**

- Did you do everything in the list in **E**?
- Is your grammar, spelling, and punctuation correct?
- Is your writing clear and easy for other people to understand?

G **Now write the final draft of your review in your notebook.**

Report

A **Read the report. Label the different sections.**

A Green Diet: How Animals Have Adapted To Eating Leaves

Many animals are herbivores that only eat leaves. Leaves are a convenient food source, but they are not very nutritious, and that makes a green diet challenging. To overcome this challenge, animals have developed many interesting adaptations.

Giraffes

Giraffes have long necks, so they can reach leaves that other animals cannot. Their tongue is 45 cm long, and is used to grab leaves. It's very tough, so it doesn't feel pain when it's handling sharp bits of plant that most animals avoid. These adaptations help the giraffe to get enough food, because they don't have to compete for it with other species.

A giraffe's tongue

Cows

Cows have four different stomachs. When they eat grass, it goes into their first and second stomachs. But after that, it comes back into their mouth and they break it into tiny pieces with their back teeth. The grass travels between their stomachs and their mouth several times. Then it goes into their third and fourth stomachs. The cows' complex digestion system helps them to extract nutrients from their food.

The four stomachs

Sloths

Sloths have a lower body temperature than most mammals, and move more slowly. They digest their food very slowly, too, and rest or sleep for up to 20 hours a day. All these adaptations help sloths to save energy and live on a green diet with very few nutrients.

A sloth

With their various adaptations, these animals can get all the energy and nutrients that they need for a healthy life.

B **Answer the questions.**

1   How does the writer start the report?

2   How do the visuals help us to understand the report?

3   How does the writer organize the information?

C You're going to write a report on how animals have adapted. Brainstorm.
Write your ideas in the graphic organizer below.

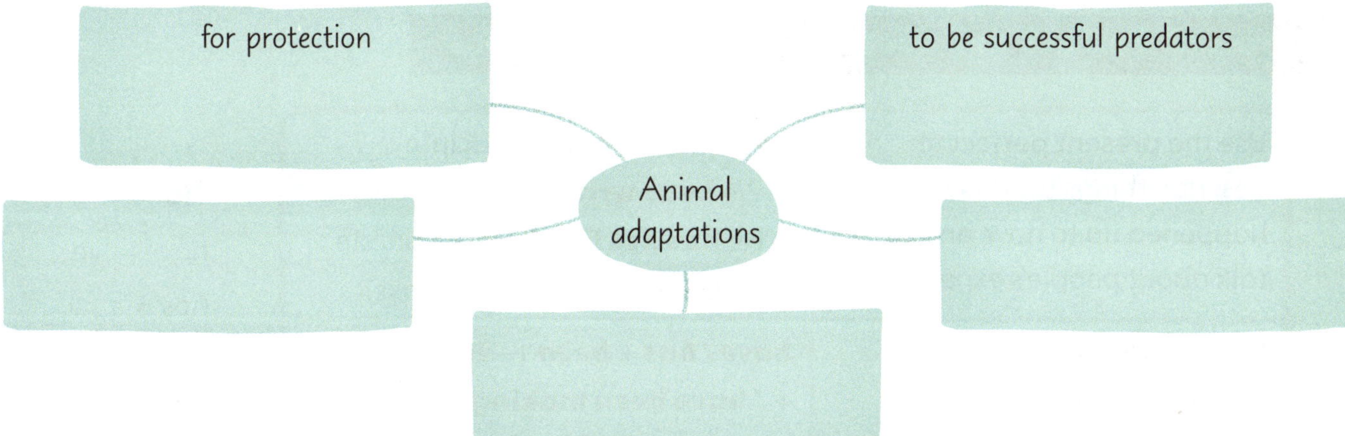

D Do some research and outline your ideas by completing the chart.

Title:		
Introduction:		
Heading 1: _____________ **Information:**	**Heading 2:** _____________ **Information:**	**Heading 3:** _____________ **Information:**
Conclusion:		

E Now write the first draft of your report in your notebook.

- Include a title that clearly states the topic and gets people interested.
- Start your report by giving some background information about the topic.
- Use visuals (pictures or diagrams) to help show the information in your report.
- Organize your report into sections with headings so it's easier to understand.
- Finish with a conclusion that summarizes the information in the report.

F Check your work and make any necessary changes.

- Did you do everything in the list in **E**?
- Is your grammar, spelling, and punctuation correct?
- Is your writing clear and easy for other people to understand?

G Now write the final draft of your report in your notebook.

Grammar Reference

Unit 1

Present Perfect and Present Perfect Continuous

		Tip
Use the **present perfect** to describe things that have happened up to now, and to talk about people's experiences.	*have / has* + past participle + We **have written** a story. – He **has not finished** the puzzle. ? **Have** you **read** many books?	have = 've has = 's have not = haven't has not = hasn't
Use the **present perfect continuous** to say that something started in the past and is still happening now.	*have / has* + *been* + *-ing* + I **have been making** new friends. – They **have not been studying**. ? **Have** you **been dancing**?	

- The past participle of most verbs is the same as the simple past form.
- Some irregular verbs have a different past participle form (see page 184).

Use *for* with a period of time: **She's been learning Japanese for three years.**

Use *since* with a moment in the past: **We've been chatting since 7:00 p.m.**

Unit 2

Review of Tenses

Use the **simple present** for things that happen regularly.	+ The bird **comes** every day and we **feed** it. – The squirrel **doesn't eat** meat. ? **Do** you usually **bike** to school?
Use the **present continuous** for things that are happening now.	+ I **am watching** the dolphins at the moment. – We **aren't testing** their intelligence now. ? **Is** the crow **thinking**?
Use the **simple past** for things that happened in the past.	+ I **photographed** the monkeys a year ago. – They **didn't find** any food yesterday. ? **Did** you **see** the nest last week?
Use the **past continuous** for what was happening at a time in the past.	+ I **was waiting** for two hours. – You **weren't sitting** in the right place. ? **Was** the gorilla **communicating** with you?

- For present perfect and present perfect continuous, see Unit 1.

Unit 3

Modals of Ability

Use **can** and **can't / cannot** to talk about the ability to do something in the **present**.	**can / can't / cannot** + base form + The computer **can speak to you**. - Robots **can't feel emotions**.
Use **could** and **couldn't / could not** to talk about the ability to do something in the **past**.	**can / can't / cannot** + base form + The computer **can speak to you**. - Robots **can't feel emotions**.
Use **will be able to** and **won't be able to / will not be able to** to talk about the ability to do something in the **future**.	**will / won't / will not** + **be able to** + base form + Cars **will be able to drive** without drivers. - A robot **won't be able to think** like a human.

Unit 4

Modals of Certainty and Possibility

Use **might** when you are **not sure if something is true**.

Use **must** and **have to / has to** when you are **sure that something is true**.

They **have to be** the coolest statues I've ever seen. The artist **must be** very talented.

The lines in the rock **might show** a lion, or they **might show** a dog. I'm not sure.

Use **can't** when you are **sure that something is NOT true**.

That building **can't be** very old. It wasn't there two years ago.

Unit 5

will and going to

Use **will** and **won't / will not**: • to talk about **facts** in the future. • to make predictions about things that you believe.	**will / won't** + base form + In 2090, we **will be old**. - I **won't win**. Other people are better. ? **Will** she **have** fun at the party?
Use **going to**: • to talk about **future plans**. • to make predictions about things that you see.	**am / is / are** + **going to** + base form + I **'m going to meet** my friends at the park. - It **isn't going to rain**. It's not cloudy. ? **Are** we **going to visit** them this summer?

Unit 6

Future with Present Continuous

Use the present continuous to talk about **future arrangements**, especially when you mention a specific time or place.

> After school on Tuesday, I**'m getting** a haircut. (You have an appointment.)

> Bella and I **are meeting** at the swimming pool at 11:00 a.m. (You have already decided where and when.)

Unit 7

Reported Speech with *Said that*

You can say what someone said using direct speech, with quotation marks around the person's words.

> **"I'm at an art museum,"** said Felix.

Alternatively, you can use reported speech to say what someone said.

> **Felix said that he was at an art museum.**

- Use *said that* to introduce the reported speech.
- If the verb is in a present tense, change it to a past tense.
- Don't use quotation marks.

Direct Speech	Reported Speech
Simple present "I **love** that painting."	**Simple past** He **said that** he **loved** that painting.
Present continuous "We **are making** a picture from leaves."	**Past continuous** They **said that** they **were making** a picture from leaves.
can "I **can't** draw well."	*could* He **said that** he **couldn't** draw well.

Tip

You often have to change the pronoun as well as the tense.

> **We** often take photos. → They said that **they** often took photos.

> **My** camera is new. → She said that **her** camera was new.

Unit 8

Use **said that** in reported speech if you don't say who the person was talking to.

"Belgian chocolate is tasty." → Francisco **said that** Belgian chocolate was tasty.

Use **told** in reported speech when you say who the person was talking to. Use someone's name or an object pronoun after **told**.

"Small green peppers are hot." → Francisco **told me that** small green peppers were hot.

Use **asked** to report questions.

asked + name or object pronoun + **if** or **whether** or question word

"Are the lemons sour?" → Francisco **asked them if** the lemons were sour.

In reported questions, use the same word order as a normal affirmative sentence.

"Where is the festival?" → I **asked** her where **the festival was**.

"Do you like cooking?" → He **asked** you whether **you liked cooking**.

Remember!

If the verb is in a present tense in direct speech, it usually changes to a past tense in reported speech.

Unit 9

You can ask questions with **who**, **what**, **where**, **when**, **why**, **which**, and **how** to get information.

Use **subject questions** when you want to know who or what does the action, but don't use *do*, *does*, or *did*.

Who helped Malumbo? Bukata helped Malumbo.

In a subject question, the question word is the subject of the question.

Use **object questions** when you want to know who or what receives the action and use **do**, **does**, or **did** before the subject.

Who did Malumbo **help**? Malumbo helped Bukata.

In an object question, the question word is the object of the question.

Unit 10

Short Answers

We often use short forms to answer *yes / no* questions. Using a short answer is often more polite than just saying *Yes* or *No*. Short answers can also avoid repetition.
To make short answers, use the first verb from the question.

Question	Short Answer	
Do they always wear a helmet?	Yes, they do.	No, they don't.
Are we going to the skatepark?	Yes, we are.	No, we aren't.
Did you learn a new trick?	Yes, I did.	No, I didn't.
Was he having fun?	Yes, he was.	No, he wasn't.
Has it been raining?	Yes, it has.	No, it hasn't.
Can she skateboard?	Yes, she can.	No, she can't.
Will they win the competition?	Yes, they will.	No, they won't.

Tip

Use the long form (no apostrophes) in affirmative answers.

Yes, I am. (NOT Yes, I'm.)

Use the short form (with apostrophes) in negative answers.

No, I'm not.

Unit 11

Present Passive

We can say the same things in two different ways by using active or passive sentences.

Active: Someone cleans the exhibits every day.

Passive: The exhibits are cleaned every day.

In the active sentence, the focus is on the person who cleans. In the passive sentence, the focus is on the exhibits.

We often use the passive if:

- we don't know exactly who or what does something.
- the "who" or "what" isn't important.
- the action is more important than the "who" or "what".

Make the present passive with **subject + *am / is / are* + past participle**.

- The past participle of most verbs is the same as the simple past form.
- Some irregular verbs have a different past participle form (see page 184).

Active	Passive
People sometimes **find** an old coin.	An old coin **is** sometimes **found**.
Someone **displays** signs about the exhibits.	Signs **are displayed** about the exhibits.

Unit 12

Past Passive

Make the past passive with **subject** + **was / were** + **past participle**.

Active	Passive
Someone **sent** the messages.	The messages **were sent**.
People **collected** the space junk.	The space junk **was collected**.
Nerea **discovered** a new planet.	A new planet **was discovered** by Nerea.

Tip

Use *by* to say who or what does the action in a passive sentence.

Active   **Passive**

School groups <u>visit</u> the museum. → The museum <u>is visited</u> **by school groups**.

Unit 13

Adjectives and Adverbs

Adjectives tell you more about nouns.

You usually put adjectives before nouns.

   The big plant has purple flowers.

With the verb *to be*, adjectives can also go after the verb.

   The flowers are small and delicate.

Adverbs can tell you more about verbs.

An **adverb of manner** tells you how something happens. It normally goes after the verb.

   He stopped suddenly when he spotted the rare plant, and studied it carefully.

Most adverbs of manner end in *-ly*, but some, e.g. *fast* and *hard*, have the same form as the adjective.

   Many desert plants grow fast after rain.

An **adverb of frequency** tells you how often something happens. It normally goes before the verb, but it goes after the verb *be*.

   That tree often <u>produces</u> nuts.   There <u>are</u> never nuts on the tree in the spring.

Adverbs can also tell you more about adjectives.

   We were incredibly thirsty after our walk through the desert.

Unit 14

Second Conditional

Use the second conditional to talk about unreal situations in the present and unlikely situations in the future.

Second conditionals have two clauses:

If clause   +   **main clause**

If + simple past   +   **would / wouldn't** + base form

The **if** clause can come before or after the main clause.

Unreal situations in the present:

If we lived in a different part of the world, **we would eat** different food. (But we don't live in a different part of the world.)

Farmers wouldn't grow potatoes **if people didn't want** to eat them. (But people do want to eat potatoes, so farmers do grow them.)

Unlikely situations in the future:

If everyone became vegetarian, **we wouldn't see** many cows in the fields. (It's unlikely that everyone will become vegetarian, so we will probably see many cows in the fields.)

Tip

When the *if* clause comes first, use a comma.

When the main clause comes first, don't use a comma.

Unit 15

Sense Verb + Adjective

With sense verbs (**look**, **feel**, **sound**, **smell**, **taste**), we use an adjective, not an adverb, to describe the verb.

Life in the circus sounds <u>exciting</u>. (NOT Life in the circus sounds excitingly.)

The trapeze doesn't feel <u>safe</u>. (NOT The trapeze doesn't feel safely.)

He looked <u>tired</u>. (NOT He looked tiredly.)

The flowers smelled <u>beautiful</u>! (NOT The flowers smelled beautifully!)

Unit 16

Infinitives and Gerunds with Adjectives

Use **it's** + **adjective** + **infinitive** to express an opinion.

It's fun to daydream. **It isn't difficult to write a poem.**

You can say the same thing with a gerund (*-ing*) at the beginning of the sentence:

Daydreaming is fun. **Writing a poem isn't difficult.**

Use these patterns with adjectives such as *difficult*, *easy*, *right*, *wrong*, *nice*, *fun*, in any tense.

Unit 17

A, An, The, and No Article

Use **a** or **an** the first time you talk about something. Use **the** when you talk about it again.

I have an allergy to nuts. The allergy can be dangerous.

Use **a** and **an** with things that aren't special.

I wrote a story about an astronaut.

Use **a** and **an** for jobs.

I want to be an actor or a singer.

Use **the** when the person you're talking to knows what you're talking about.

I've met a lot of nice people at the club.

Don't use an article to talk about sports, meals, most countries, and school subjects.

I love history and basketball. **What do people in China eat for lunch?**

Don't use an article with plural nouns when you're talking about things in general.

I like acting in plays. **Telescopes help you see things far away.**

Unit 18

Review of Tenses and Future Forms

For the simple present, present continuous, simple past, past continuous, present perfect, and present perfect continuous, see page 176.

For **will** and **going to**, see page 177.

For the future with present continuous, see page 178.

Irregular Verbs

Base Form	Past Simple	Past Participle
be	was / were	been
become	became	become
begin	began	begun
bend	bent	bent
bite	bit	bitten
break	broke	broken
breed	bred	bred
bring	brought	brought
build	built	built
buy	bought	bought
catch	caught	caught
choose	chose	chosen
come	came	come
cost	cost	cost
cut	cut	cut
do	did	done
draw	drew	drawn
drink	drank	drunk
drive	drove	driven
eat	ate	eaten
fall	fell	fallen
feed	fed	fed
feel	felt	felt
find	found	found
fit	fit	fit
fly	flew	flown
get	got	gotten
give	gave	given
go	went	gone
grow	grew	grown
hang	hung	hung
have	had	had
hear	heard	heard
hide	hid	hidden
hit	hit	hit
hold	held	held
hurt	hurt	hurt
keep	kept	kept
know	knew	known
lead	led	led
leave	left	left
let	let	let

Base Form	Past Simple	Past Participle
lie	lay	lain
light	lit	lit
lose	lost	lost
make	made	made
meet	met	met
overcome	overcame	overcome
pay	paid	paid
put	put	put
quit	quit	quit
read	read	read
ride	rode	ridden
ring	rang	rung
rise	rose	risen
run	ran	run
say	said	said
see	saw	seen
sell	sold	sold
send	sent	sent
set	set	set
show	showed	shown
shut	shut	shut
sing	sang	sung
sit	sat	sat
sleep	slept	slept
speak	spoke	spoken
spend	spent	spent
stand	stood	stood
stink	stank	stunk
sweep	swept	swept
swim	swam	swum
take	took	taken
teach	taught	taught
tear	tore	torn
tell	told	told
think	thought	thought
throw	threw	thrown
understand	understood	understood
wake up	woke up	woken up
wear	wore	worn
win	won	won
write	wrote	written